TRUMPCOIN

MAKE CRYPTO GREAT AGAIN

A DECENTRALISED CRYPTOCURRENCY
PART OF THE "ALT-ERNATIVE" BOOK SERIES

TrumpCoin—Make Crypto Great Again

by Christopher P. Thompson

Copyright © 2016 by Christopher P. Thompson

All rights reserved.

Book Author by Christopher P. Thompson

Book Design by C. Ellis

No part of this book may be reproduced in any written, electronic, recording, or photocopying without written permission of the publisher or author. The exception would be in the case of brief quotations embodied in the critical articles or reviews, images and pages where permission is specifically granted by the publisher or author.

Although every precaution has been taken to verify the accuracy of the information contained herein, the author and publisher assume no responsibility for any errors or omissions. No liability is assumed for damages that may result from the use of information contained within.

ISBN—13: 978—1539755395
ISBN—10: 1539755398

TRUMPCOIN

MAKE CRYPTO GREAT AGAIN

A DECENTRALISED CRYPTOCURRENCY
PART OF THE "ALT-ERNATIVE" BOOK SERIES

CHRISTOPHER P. THOMPSON

ABOUT THE AUTHOR

Christopher Paul Thompson is an avid cryptocurrency enthusiast from the United Kingdom. Born in Bradford, UK and academically educated at the University of York (BSc Mathematics). He has been a keen follower of past and current events in the crypto space since March 2013. His first book called Cryptocurrency "The Alt-ernative" A Beginner's Reference is the first book he has ever written.

Other titles currently available:

"Peercoin—History of the First Year"
"Reddcoin—History of the First Year"
"DigiByte—History of the First Year"
"Dogecoin—History of the First Year"
"GoldCoin—History of the First Year"
"Digitalcoin—History of the First Year"
"Crypto Bullion—History of the First Year"

Other titles to be released soon:

"Anoncoin—History of the First Year"
"Yocoin—History of the First Year"
"Diamond—An Extended History"
"Mooncoin—Philosophy of Decentralisation"
"Unobtanium—An Extended History"
"Sativacoin—An Extended History"

E-mail Contact: chris_thompson25@live.co.uk
Twitter Contact: https://twitter.com/MrSilverCider

CONTENTS

Introduction	10-11
What is TrumpCoin?	12
Why use TrumpCoin?	13
Is TrumpCoin Money?	14
TrumpCoin Specification	15
TrumpCoin Milestone Timeline	16-18
Ten Donald Trump Quotes	19
TrumpCoin Blockchain	20-21
Proof of Work (PoW) Mining	22
What is Proof of Work/Stake?	23
TrumpCoin Development Team	24-25
TrumpCoin Wallets	26
TrumpCoin Exchanges	27
View of User "Bitbobb"	28-31
View of User "Depredation"	32
TrumpCoin Community	33
History of TrumpCoin	35
Launch of the TrumpCoin Blockchain (FEBRUARY 2016)	37-43
GOP Primary/Caucus Results (FEBRUARY 2016)	44
Venues of Trump's Speeches (FEBRUARY 2016)	45
Founder Considered Leaving TrumpCoin as the Value of the Coin Slid (MARCH 2016)	47-56
GOP Primary/Caucus Results (MARCH 2016)	57-58
Venues of Trump's Speeches (MARCH 2016)	59

CONTENTS

Transition to the New PoS Blockchain (APRIL 2016)	....	61-69
GOP Primary/Caucus Results (APRIL 2016)	....	70
Venues of Trump's Speeches (APRIL 2016)	....	71
TrumpCoin Promotional Video Uploaded to YouTube (MAY 2016)	....	73-81
GOP Primary/Caucus Results (MAY 2016)	....	82
Venues of Trump's Speeches (MAY2016)	....	83
Founder of TrumpCoin Resigned from the Lead Project Manager Role (JUNE 2016)	....	85-93
GOP Primary/Caucus Results (JUNE 2016)	....	94
Venues of Trump's Speeches (JUNE 2016)	....	95
A New TrumpCoin LLC Team Established (JULY 2016)	....	97-108
Venues of Trump's Speeches (JULY 2016)	....	109
Further Promotion of TrumpCoin (AUGUST 2016)	....	111-118
Venues of Trump's Speeches (AUGUST 2016)	....	119
High Risks Attributed to Donating the Trump Fund to a Political Campaign (SEPTEMBER 2016)	....	121-126
Venues of Trump's Speeches (SEPTEMBER 2016)	....	127
Eight Months of TrumpCoin (OCTOBER 2016)	....	129-132
Venues of Trump's Speeches (OCTOBER 2016)	....	133
APPENDIX	....	135
Introducing TrumpCoin Article	....	137-139
TrumpCoin Aims to Make Crypto Great Again Article	....	141-143

INTRODUCTION

Cryptocurrency was born with the advent of Bitcoin. It was first mentioned in a research paper published online titled "Bitcoin: A Peer-to-Peer Electronic Cash System" with the real name or pseudonym Satoshi Nakamoto attributed to it. This paper was published on the 31st of October 2008. About two months later on the 3rd of January 2009, the Bitcoin network protocol was launched. This technological breakthrough was the beginning of a decentralized public ledger. It allows people to send value across the globe without the permission of a third party authority.

Since then, a growing number of people around the world have been introduced to or discovered cryptocurrency. Many cryptocurrencies have been launched over the following years since the introduction of Bitcoin. The name "alternative" was given to these cryptocurrencies after Bitcoin because they were developed, implemented and introduced to be used instead of or alongside Bitcoin. One could say, a choice of brand in cryptocurrency exists. People have discovered these either through word of mouth, by accident, through personal investigation or via the media. Nevertheless, it has changed the lives of many people. It has provoked the general public into asking innumerable questions about many issues based on subjects such as economics, politics, philosophy, mathematics and so on.

In this book, I hope to give the reader insight into how one particular alternative cryptocurrency began. TrumpCoin began in February 2016 as a X11 (hashing algorithm) proof of work cryptocurrency. This book, as well as other future books to be written on other cryptocurrencies, is a historical story of the first eight months from the 17th of February to the 17th of October 2016. It also describes the terminology one encounters in cryptocurrency such as proof of work mining, block reward, wallets and so on.

INTRODUCTION

I chose to write about just the first eight months for various reasons, some of which are:

- For almost all cryptocurrencies, the first period of their existence is the most defining period.
- If I had chosen to write a full history of TrumpCoin, I would be continuously playing catch up.
- Currently I have a full-time job besides being a cryptocurrency author, so my time is unfortunately limited.
- Ultimately, I wanted the book to be published a couple of weeks before the US Presidential General Election.

You may have bought this book because TrumpCoin is your favourite cryptocurrency. Alternatively, you may be keen to find out how it all began. I have presented the information henceforth without going into too much technical discussion about TrumpCoin. If you would like to investigate further, I recommend that you read material currently available online at the official website at http://trumpcoin.com/.

If you choose to purchase a certain amount of TrumpCoin, please do not buy more than you can afford to lose.

Enjoy the book :D

WHAT IS TRUMPCOIN?

TrumpCoin is a cryptocurrency or digital decentralised currency used via the Internet. It is described as a payment network without the need for a central authority such as a bank or other central clearing house. It allows the end user to store or transfer value anywhere in the world with the use of a personal computer, laptop or smartphone. Cryptography has been implemented and coded into the network allowing the user to send currency through a decentralised (no centre point of failure), open source (anyone can review the code), peer-to-peer network. Cryptography also controls the creation of newly minted units of TRUMP account.

In January 2014, Richard Wagner (an elementary school teacher in Madison, WI) began a short-lived project to introduce cryptocurrency into politics. He created the BVPAC (Bitcoin Voter's Political Action Committee) Project that influenced the FEC (Federal Election Commission) to accommodate cryptocurrencies in political donation activities. However, this only lasted for a few days due to regulations at both the state and federal level. TrumpCoin seeks to fulfil the objective set out by the BVPAC, but this time succeed. TrumpCoin's objective, working directly with industry experts in the crypto space, politics, and media, is to make cryptocurrencies more acceptable as a means to raise money for election campaigns.

On the official website at http://trumpcoin.com, TrumpCoin is described as:

"TrumpCoin is a political movement by the people, coming together to secure a bright future for Donald Trump's presidential campaign."

The slogan used by the TrumpCoin community to market the coin is:

"THE WORLD'S FIRST DECENTRALIZED CRYPTOPAC"

WHY USE TRUMPCOIN?

Like all cryptocurrencies, people have chosen to adopt TrumpCoin as a medium of exchange or store of wealth through personal choice. An innovative feature of the coin, an affinity towards the brand or high confidence of the community could be reasons why they have done so. Key benefits of using TrumpCoin are:

- It is a useful medium of exchange via which value can be transferred internationally for a fraction of the cost of other conventional methods.

- TrumpCoin eliminates the need for a trusted third party such as a bank, clearing house or other centralised authority (e.g. PayPal). All transactions are solely from one person to another (peer-to-peer).

- TrumpCoin has the potential to engage people worldwide who are without a bank account (unbanked).

- TrumpCoin is immune from the effects of hyperinflation, unlike the current fiat monetary systems around the world.

When the TrumpCoin network protocol launched in February 2016, a certain number of TRUMP were put aside called the Trump Fund. Its history is sufficiently documented in the history chapters of this book. The ultimate aim is to see this fund increase in value as more investors buy the coin. The developers were happy to point out that, unlike a donation where you never see your money again, you would still hold valuable TRUMP.

In conclusion, one would be supporting the value of the Trump Fund in order to create a large donation towards the campaign before and after November.

IS TRUMPCOIN MONEY?

Money is a form of acceptable, convenient and valued medium of payment for goods and services within an economy. It allows two parties to exchange goods or services without the need to barter. This eradicates the potential situation where one party of the two may not want what the other has to offer. The main properties of money are:

- **As a medium of exchange**—money can be used as a means to buy/sell goods/services without the need to barter.
- **A unit of account**—a common measure of value wherever one is in the world.
- **Portable**—easily transferred from one party to another. The medium used can be easily carried.
- **Durable**—all units of the currency can be lost, but not destroyed.
- **Divisible**—each unit can be subdivided into smaller fractions of that unit.
- **Fungible**— each unit of account is the same as every other unit within the medium (1 TRUMP = 1 TRUMP)
- **As a store of value**—it sustains its purchasing power (what it can buy) over long periods of time.

TrumpCoin easily satisfies the first six characteristics. Taking into account the last characteristic, the value of TrumpCoin, like all currencies, comes from people willing to accept it as a medium of exchange for payment of goods or services. As it gets adopted by more individuals or merchants, its intrinsic value will increase accordingly.

TRUMPCOIN SPECIFICATION

Since the launch of TrumpCoin, its coin specification has changed a few times. At the time of publication of this book, its current specification is:

Coin Symbol:	TRUMP
Unit of account:	TRUMP
Date of Announcement:	17th of February 2016
Block Number One Generated:	21st of February 2016
Founder:	user "chicken65"
Lead Developer:	user "Signal7"
Hashing Algorithm:	Blake-256
Timestamping Algorithm:	Proof of Stake
Address Begins With:	T
Total Coins:	12 million TRUMP
Block Time:	Unknown
Difficulty Retarget Time:	Unknown
Annual Inflation:	~2%
Confirmations per Transaction:	Unknown
Pre-mine:	3.5% (700,000 TRUMP)

TRUMPCOIN MILESTONE TIMELINE

17th of February 2016	—Original TrumpCoin Bitcointalk thread created.
17th of February 2016	—First official Twitter account for the coin was created at http://twitter.com/trumpcoin1.
20th of February 2016	—Original scheduled public launch failed (surpassed).
21st of February 2016	—Mining of TrumpCoin began slightly after midnight.
28th of February 2016	—Vixtrade was the first exchange to initiate trades of TrumpCoin on its platform.
28th of February 2016	—User "logocreator" won the logo competition.
28th of February 2016	—YoBit was the second exchange to initiate trades of TrumpCoin on its platform.
1st of March 2016	—TrumpCoin added to www.coimarketcap.com.
6th of March 2016	—Trump Fund transferred over to user "indiemax".
7th of March 2016	—Safecex was the third exchange to initiate trades of TrumpCoin on its platform.
15th of March 2016	—Total number of TRUMP surpassed 5 million.
19th of March 2016	—User "chicken65" thought about abandoning the coin.
6th of April 2016	—First known independent article written about the coin by Vocativ.
11th of April 2016	—block number one of the new PoS blockchain was timestamped at 11:01 UTC.
12th of April 2016	—C-Cex was the fourth exchange to initiate trades of TrumpCoin on its platform.
13th of April 2016	—Subreddit at .../r/trumpcoin was founded.
17th of April 2016	—C-Cex introduced the TRUMP/USD trading pair.

TRUMPCOIN MILESTONE TIMELINE

1st of May 2016	—Efforts were being made to get TrumpCoin noticed by the official Trump campaign team.
17th of May 2016	—A 15,000 TRUMP bounty campaign to create a "How To Consumer Site" was issued by user "chicken65".
25th of May 2016	—Promotional video titled "Introducing: TrumpCoin?" uploaded to YouTube by user "TrumpCoinContent".
28th of May 2016	—Cryptopia was the sixth exchange to initiate trades of TrumpCoin on its platform.
1st of June 2016	—Promotional video titled "What is TrumpCoin?" uploaded to YouTube by user "TrumpCoinContent".
15th of June 2016	—User "chicken65" announced his resignation.
16th of June 2016	—User "CantStump" selected as the new lead project manager of TrumpCoin.
27th of June 2016	—The website domain http://trumpcoin.com was secured by user "bitbullbarbados".
30th of June 2016	—Market capitalisation of the coin surpassed one million US Dollars for the first time.
1st of July 2016	—All time high market capitalisation of the coin was attained at roughly $1,243,470.
11th of July 2016	—TrumpCoin became a limited liability company, LLC.
14th of July 2016	—User "Signal7" became Temporary Chariman.
19th of July 2016	—A new dedicated TrumpCoin block explorer was created at http://chain.blockpioneers.info/trump.
19th of July 2016	—User "DreadLordColi" became temporary treasurer.
24th of July 2016	—A new TrumpCoin Team had been assembled.

TRUMPCOIN MILESTONE TIMELINE

2nd of August 2016	—A statement issued by the founder of TrumpCoin.
2nd of August 2016	—TrumpCoin began to be powered by PayServices.
3rd of August 2016	—Video titled "MAGA: Join The Fight For America" uploaded to YouTube.
5th of August 2016	—User "Skirmant" launched a TRUMP Reddit TipBot.
12th of August 2016	—Last post by user "Signal7" during the month.
19th of August 2016	—an independent article was published about the coin titled "TrumpCoin Aims to Make Crypto Great Again".
24th of August 2016	—A new dedicated TrumpCoin block explorer was created at http://blockexperts.com/trump.
9th of September 2016	—User "DreadLordColi" resigned from his role as the temporary treasurer on the official TrumpCoin Team.
16th of September 2016	—Complications existed in regards to being able to give the Trump Fund to the Trump campaign team.
25th of September 2016	—User "Skirmant" launched a TRUMP Twitter TipBot.
4th of October 2016	—A brief description of TrumpCoin sent to Breitbart.
12th October 2016	—A video titled "Donald Trump—The Alpha Male" was uploaded to YouTube by user "yaooke".
15th of October 2016	—User "chicken65" believed there was still life in the TrumpCoin project.
17th of October 2016	—No posts submitted by user "Signal7" for over one month.
17th of October 2016	—Twenty two days until the US Presidential General Election.

TEN DONALD TRUMP QUOTES

"My IQ is one of the highest — and you all know it! Please don't feel so stupid or insecure; it's not your fault."

"We are not talking about isolation, we are talking about security. We are not talking about religion, we are talking about security."

"He's not a war hero — he's a war hero because he was captured. I like people that weren't captured."

"I'm Donald Trump. I wrote "The Art Of The Deal". I say that not in a braggadocious way."

"We, as a country, either have borders or we don't. If we don't have borders, we don't have a country."

"I will be the greatest jobs president that God ever created."

"Sometimes your best investments are the ones you don't make."

"All of the women on The Apprentice flirted with me - consciously or unconsciously. That's to be expected."

"What separates the winners from the losers is how a person reacts to each new twist of fate."

"I think the big problem this country has is being politically correct. I've been challenged by so many people, and I don't frankly have time for total political correctness. And to be honest with you, this country doesn't have time either."

"Part of being a winner is knowing when enough is enough. Sometimes you have to give up the fight and walk away, and move on to something that's more productive."

TRUMPCOIN BLOCKCHAIN

Every cryptocurrency has a corresponding blockchain within its decentralised network protocol. TrumpCoin is no different in this sense. A blockchain is simply described as a general public ledger of all transactions and blocks ever executed since the very first block. In addition, it continuously updates in real time each time a new block is successfully mined/minted. Blocks enter the blockchain in such a manner that each block contains the hash of the previous one. It is therefore utterly resistant to modification along the chain since each block is related to the prior one. Consequently, the problem of doubling-spending is solved.

As a means for the general public to view the blockchain, web developers have created block explorers. The first block explorer for TrumpCoin was made available at the domain http://173.44.41.235/index.php just two hours before the public launch of the blockchain. It was announced as being accessible on the 20th of February 2016. However, it no longer exists.

In April, the developers decided to transition to a totally new blockchain which they viewed as more promising over the long term. Users had to swap their old V1 TRUMP for new V2 TRUMP before a specific deadline. Instead of the timestamping being proof of work, it had become solely proof of stake.

Since the inception of the first block explorer, other websites have been created. Currently there are two reliable block explorers for the coin at:

- http://chain.blockpioneers.info/trump/explorer.php;
- https://www.blockexperts.com/trump;

These two block explorers only have the open public ledger record of all blocks and transactions since the launch of the new blockchain. It is difficult to find any records attaining to the block history of the first blockchain (V1 Blockchain).

TRUMPCOIN BLOCKCHAIN

Block explorers tend to present different layouts, statistics and charts. Some are more extensive in terms of the information given. Some statistics include:

- **Height of block** —the block number of the network.
- **Time of block** —the time at which the block was timestamped to the blockchain.
- **Transactions** —the number of transactions in that particular block.
- **Total Sent** —the total amount of cryptocurrency sent in that particular block.
- **Block Reward** —how many coins were generated in the block (added to the overall coin circulation).

Below is a screenshot of block number one of the V2 Blockchain from the block explorer at https://www.blockexperts.com/trump/

TRUMPCOIN BLOCK #1
block hash 0001a6ef53ebaa84acc5c4fb5478aa52bb62d57d50b464f939604102ce33b422

Timestamp	2016-04-11 13:01:32	Miner	Unknown
Height	1	Transactions	1
Difficulty	3.81E-6	Total Ouput	6500000.00000000 TRUMP
Version	6	Fees	0.00000000 TRUMP
Bits	1f03ffff	Block Reward	6500000.00000000 TRUMP
Nonce	956301440	Show raw block	
Size	174.00000 B		

PROOF OF WORK (PoW) MINING

Proof of work mining is a competitive computerised process which helps to maintain and secure the blockchain in such a way as to verify transactions and prevent double spending.

In the general sense of cryptocurrency, those who participate in the activity of mining are called miners. They are general members of the cryptocurrency community who dedicate processing power (hash) of their computers towards solving highly complex mathematical problems and verifying transactions. This process upholds the integrity and security of the network. As such, miners are described as protectors of the network. Each transaction (held within a certain block) is validated before adding it to the blockchain. By doing this, they are rewarded (as an incentive) with newly generated mined coins or transaction fees. These coins are issued by the software in a transparent and predictable way outside of the control of its founders and developers. A miner can be based anywhere in the world as long as they have an internet connection, sufficient knowledge of how one mines and the hardware/software required to do so.

Miners use GPUs (Graphical Processing Units) or CPUs (Central Processing Units) to process transactions by hashing. Also, Application Specific Integrated Circuits (ASICs) allow miners to use customised hardware for faster and lower power mining.

Initially, the timestamping algorithm of TrumpCoin was solely proof of work. On the 11th of April, the new V2 Blockchain launched and became publicly available to users four days later at 13:00 UTC.

WHAT IS PROOF OF WORK/STAKE?

Proof of work and proof of stake are both referred to collectively as timestamping methods. They are the methods used to secure the network protocol of a certain cryptocurrency in order to sustain decentralisation and validate transactions. Therefore, no third party needs to be trusted to verify and then add transactions the blockchain.

Proof of work mining is currently used in the decentralised network protocol of Bitcoin thanks to the research by Satoshi Nakamoto. Miners commit the processing (hashing) power of their computers towards successfully finding blocks either individually or as part of a group with other miners (mining pool). As the cumulative hash of the network increases, the network becomes more secure.

Proof of stake was independently discovered by Sunny King after he studied the work of Nakamoto. It was introduced into Peercoin alongside proof of work on the 19th of August 2012. Users of the wallet client help to secure the network by keeping their clients active. When coins arrive in a given wallet address, they begin to age and, after a certain time period, a number of coins are rewarded.

Proof of stake is widely accepted as the environmentally friendly way to timestamp transactions to the blockchain instead of the high energy cost of proof of work.

TRUMPCOIN DEVELOPMENT TEAM

Jason Bobbitt (Lead Developer & Chief Technical Officer)

"Our fearless leader Jason (who goes by Signal7 in the community) has made some amazing progress in the TrumpCoin developmental process. His most recent order of business was to make TrumpCoin, well, a business. Jason registered TrumpCoin as an LLC in early July and began forming a team of people to fit all the necessary roles to ensure the success of TrumpCoin for years to come. Jason works in the tech sector for an industry-leading company and is passionate about cryptocurrency in politics. As our CTO, he can be reached for any technical questions, problems or suggestions."

Robert Wurzer (Community Outreach)

Robert AKA "Depredation" has been with TrumpCoin since day one. He got involved with cryptocurrencies in 2013 as a member of the DogeCoin community and has noticed several similarities between the two coins in terms of the possibilities of media attention, but believes TrumpCoin's ceiling is infinitely higher. We wanted to add members to the team that would be especially dedicated to making sure that the community was always "in the loop" - Robert was perfect for the job. Robert can be found in various forums answering questions, in chat rooms engaging in Q&A, and much, more. Robert is a biology student at UC Santa Barbara and an absolutely brilliant mind that we were honored to bring on to the team.

Alex B. (Social Media Coordinator)

Alex has run some form of a social media campaign on just about every platform there is, beginning in 2014. He officially joined the TrumpCoin team in July of 2016 as the Social Media Coordinator and, along with a team of dedicated media managers, Alex helps ensure that the TrumpCoin project's public presence is professional, informative, and engaging to the curious investor and the long-term supporter alike!

TRUMPCOIN DEVELOPMENT TEAM

Alex is based out of Chicago and has supported Donald J. Trump for President since February 2016. There is no denying how big of a role social media plays in the advancement of any project this decade; which is why we decided to bring in a "ringer".

Scott H. (Ad Hoc Merchandiser)

Scott has been following cryptocurrency since the times of e-gold, predating Bitcoin. He studied international business and has an analytical mind that loves to solve complex problems. Bitbobb was naturally lead to Bitcoin, and other altcoins, before finally finding his new home with TrumpCoin. We are pleased to have him and his never-say-die attitude as a merchandising associate. Scott strives to be known as the innovator who put the "goods" back into "goods and services." You should expect to see some breathtaking TrumpCoin shirts available for purchase with TrumpCoins very soon!

John M. (Media Content Manager)

John has been with TrumpCoin since the beginning. He began as a fan and an investor, but we eventually managed to convince him to join the team and use his absolutely amazing video creation skills to help our project reach all types of new markets. If you have seen any of the official TrumpCoin videos, you know just how valuable someone with his abilities is to the success of TrumpCoin! John will be creating media in alignment with marketing, videos about the project and much, much, more. John is an Australian, currently working on a TV pilot, and is heavy into American politics (like seriously, obsessed). He's known around the community as TCC or simply "Video Guy"!

TRUMPCOIN WALLETS

A wallet is basically a piece of software that can be used on a personal computer, tablet or smartphone. It allows users to store TrumpCoin as well as execute transfers of TRUMP with other users. Alternatively, it can be described as a means to access the coins from the inseparable blockchain (public transaction ledger). The wallet cryptographically generates and holds the public and private keys necessary to make these transactions possible. The software can be accessed, downloaded and installed from the official website by clicking on the "WALLETS" option at the top of the official TrumpCoin website at http://trumpcoin.com.

Unlike many other cryptocurrencies, the developers of the coin were not interested in regular updates of the wallet client. Instead, they have been focusing on the social aspects of the coin and seeking the official endorsement from the Trump Campaign Team.

According to the official website of TrumpCoin, both a Windows and Mac OS X wallet client are available. A Linux version of the client does not exist.

TRUMPCOIN EXCHANGES

A cryptocurrency exchange is a site on which registered users can buy or sell TrumpCoin against BTC, LTC, USD and so on. Some exchanges require users to fully register by submitting certain documentation including proof of identity and address. On the other hand, most exchanges only require users to register with a simple username and password with the use of a currently held e-mail account.

During the first eight months of TrumpCoin, six exchanges decided to initiate trading of TRUMP on their platforms. Dates on which trading began on these were:

Exchange	Traded Against	Status	Date added
Vixtrade	BTC	CLOSED	28th of February 2016
YoBit	BTC	ACTIVE	28th of February 2016
Safecex	BTC	CLOSED	6th of March 2016
C-Cex	BTC, LTC, USD, DOGE and ETH	ACTIVE	12th of April 2016
Cryptopia	BTC, LTC, DOGE, XMR and so on	ACTIVE	28th of May 2016
Novaexchange	BTC, LTC, ARI and CJ	ACTIVE	Unknown

TrumpCoin has enjoyed the vast majority of trades on YoBit and C-Cex. A direct trading pair TRUMP/USD exists on C-Cex, but the volume of this pair has been extremely low. Logos of these two exchanges are:

VIEW OF USER "BITBOBB"

"I found TrumpCoin in early June, 2016. I had just decided to take some time off from work to treat my health and took the opportunity to learn how to mine Bitcoin which was something I wanted to do since 2009 when I was first told about it.

I have a crazy work life since I am cross trained in many high skill professions and so many times I must put my personal hobbies and passions on hold while I complete my obligations to my customers.

After much searching I decided to look for an alt-coin which is a Bitcoin clone of sorts for they seemed more profitable than Bitcoin. It was while doing a review of many popular alt-coins when I found TrumpCoin. I had always known about Bitcointalk forums but never had need to go there and post since I was not creating coins, or doing much of anything. However, after reading many threads there over the year, I noticed that TrumpCoin had some potential.

I decided to register and after reading all the TrumpCoin posts (which took five days) I contacted Chicken65.

So after reading the thread I decided to buy some TrumpCoin from Chicken65 and learn how to use the exchanges to buy more. I was now a TrumpCoin holder. I was shocked to learn that this crypto coin was open to community involvement since many crypto coins are not friendly to outsiders jumping in. So since then I have tried my best to help with insightful commenting on the Bitcointalk thread and by networking behind the scenes with those more involved.

Early on, Chicken65 told me I should make my own crypto coin because he saw how enthusiastic I was about crypto coins. I thought this was a mistake by him to talk me down from helping his coin and it made me suspicious. Instead I stayed with TrumpCoin for the experience it will give me and I have learned a lot I must admit.

VIEW OF USER "BITBOBB"

I learned about FUD as a way to disrupt the progress of a coin so the FUDDER can get coins cheaper. In the case of TrumpCoin, it has a dual effect to stress out the people running the development of the coin and its projects.

The main lesson learned here is that crypto coins that attempt great social and political change must be decentralized like some of the great alt-hospitals must be so that they can survive attacks from hostile governments and private groups and individuals who have a financial stake in the status-quo. The net effect is a reduction in transparency and the closest followers may be the last to know of the progress.

So now as I write this we are only days away from the most important election the USA has seen since George Washington. We must now again break away from the globalist ties that have been encroaching on this free people in the USA. And how ironic that a world money has this candidate in mind. Yet the logic becomes apparent when you consider that Jannet Yellen recently admitted that the Federal Reserve has no jurisdiction over Bitcoin and therefore TrumpCoin. So digital money is truly an opportunity to assist people in a more direct way than ever before on this planet. I wonder if the promise of digital money will get realised by the people in time before the banks populate the space and forever regulate the potential into the ground? Even with the current over regulation, Bitcoin still outperforms legacy fiat by 25% per year. If the average citizen knew these numbers, digital money would become the new reserve currency. Since those percentages are normally only available to bank owners and their rich friends.

And now again the community of TrumpCoin is struggling to push on. I am very hopeful for both the future of TrumpCoin, the USA and the world and I hope that my experiences here will assist me as I go out into the world to improve where I can.

VIEW OF USER "BITBOBB"

Thank you Tyke for writing this book. And thank you dear reader for having an interest in something so interesting that many cannot look away.

PS. The current struggles of the media with the loss of Julian Assange RIP last week (10/16/2016) will Trump the need for a new money to morph into a greater security of this new networkingthat news and money both obviously need. Wikileaks was an early example of Bitcoim being used that struck me as important and as one of the truly unbanked since 2004 that should account for something. The hope that crypto will empower folks to do more than become their own bank but also to become their own band width and production they'd realize they can choose who to support too.

Perhaps beneath this can lie a long overdue movement for increased access to the means of production at the community level which will increase innovation again. So often there are bottle necks for wealth building activities or quality of life building activities… Trump calls it jobs and the nation state model has not been disproven so the local communities need jobs to have stability and balance. Legally if we must as individuals go outside and fix our own roads each year for a while until we find trusted public servants for the job then the right of association provides we be allowed to get this job done and even moral law dictates access to the reward for a job well done. Why should Americans go out and fix our own roads if the politicians still get paid? Or how long will we stand by and watch as the infrastructure crumbles around us and we are still getting ripped off? It is time to take the jobs away from the crooked politicians, media, ad quasi-gov. agency that refuses to do their job and give it to loyal hard working Americans who love our country.

VIEW OF USER "BITBOBB"

Elections are the peaceful way we hand over power in this country and the current entrenched world mafia is hell bent on keeping the status quo and will not risk another Kennedy getting into office and helping the people. And yet, each civilization clings to the values of western civilization which can now be referred to as international law since all wish to reap the benefit from it's close adherence. And Trump by supporting the nation state model and a relaxed approach to globalism in the form of good deals represents a more friendly approach to positive international law in the long term since no good space gets populated recklessly with any immediate real satisfaction. And my hope is that awareness will lead the way to discovery of the possibility that individuals have for direct access to an orderly system that benefits all via the nation state model as upheld by over time by the enhanced individual control brought on by the ability that digital money enables. This will be the new balance of power where the people will continue to risk being enslaved by their inferiors should they refuse to participate in the process."

VIEW OF "DEPREDATION"

How did you discover TrumpCoin?
On Bitcointalk when the announcement was first released in early February.

What attracted you to TrumpCoin / cryptocurrency in general?
Cryptocurrency is so intriguing and it's "The Wild West" where anything goes and there's always something interesting going on.

How have you contributed to TrumpCoin?
I've done little things here and there over the course of TrumpCoin's existence, but I purchased two block explorers, a faucet, and an android wallet that is in the works right now.

Where do you see TrumpCoin in the short/long term?
Short term? I'm not so sure. I feel like the thing about this coin is it could randomly explode at any time However, in the long term, I believe this coin has great potential because of Dan Backer and due to the fact that even if Trump wins or loses it would still be good for the coin. If he wins, he is the president and our coin may possibly gain attention and if he loses, he would care less about the things he does or endorses and may come check out TrumpCoin. I mean it is HIS coin basically; it has his name on it.

What is your most memorable event of TrumpCoin since it launched back in February 2016?
The early July price increase. During that weekend, everyone (including me), believed that there would be a mention on the Alex Jones show and the price shot up. It was such a high energy and crazy event that I'll never forget. It gave everyone the feeling of "We're actually doing it!", but that feeling was short lived. I'm hoping it will happen again but even stronger and this time not just based on a rumor. TrumpCoin in a way is an advertisement for Trump on its own, so if it goes viral it would help out Trump a good amount. It's also a great thing to see everyone happy that the coin is doing well.

TRUMPCOIN COMMUNITY

A community is a social unit or network that shares common values and goals. It derives from the Old French word "comuntee". This, in turn, originates from "communitas" in Latin (communis; things held in common). TrumpCoin has a community consisting of an innumerable number of individuals who have the coin's well being and future goal at heart. These individuals almost always prefer fictitious names with optional corresponding "avatars". Notable members of the community are users "chicken65", "Signal7", "Bitbobb" and so on.

At the time of publication, there are social media sites on which discussion and development of TrumpCoin take place. These are:

- **Bitcointalk** -https://bitcointalk.org/index.php?topic=1558916.0
- **Facebook** -https://www.facebook.com/TrumpCoin-1261248230554491
- **Reddit** -https://www.reddit.com/r/trumpcoin
- **Twitter** -https://twitter.com/trumpcointweets
- **YouTube** -https://www.youtube.com/channel/UCrvedbf2mAUNj5aKveULVbA

In essence, the community surrounding and participating in the development of TrumpCoin is the backbone of the coin. Without a following, the prospects of future adoption and utilisation are starkly limited. TrumpCoin belongs to all those people who use it, not just to the developers who aid its progression.

HISTORY OF TRUMPCOIN

LIST OF CHAPTERS

FEBRUARY 2016	—LAUNCH OF THE TRUMPCOIN BLOCKCHAIN
MARCH 2016	—FOUNDER CONSIDERED LEAVING TRUMPCOIN AS THE VALUE OF THE COIN SLID
APRIL 2016	— TRANSITION TO THE NEW POS BLOCKCHAIN
MAY 2016	—TRUMPCOIN PROMTIONAL VIDEO UPLOADED TO YOUTUBE
JUNE 2016	—FOUNDER OF TRUMPCOIN RESIGNED FROM THE LEAD PROJECT MANAGER ROLE
JULY 2016	—A NEW TRUMPCOIN LLC TEAM ESTABLISHED
AUGUST 2016	—FURTHER PROMOTION OF TRUMPCOIN
SEPTEMBER 2016	—HIGH RISKS ATTRIBUTED TO DONATING THE TRUMP FUND TO A POLITICAL CAMPAIGN
OCTOBER 2016	—EIGHT MONTHS OF TRUMPCOIN

LAUNCH OF THE TRUMPCOIN BLOCKCHAIN
FEBRUARY 2016

I. Bitcointalk forum thread created for TrumpCoin.

II. TrumpCoin network protocol launched after pre-mine.

III. First block explorer (light) went live at http://173.44.41.235/index.php.

IV. Two exchanges initiated trading of TRUMP called Vixtrade and YoBit.

V. User "logocreator" won the coin logo design competition.

On the 17th of February 2016 at 06:20:11 UTC, a Bitcointalk forum thread was created by a user known by the fictitious forum name "chicken65". This thread was originally titled "[ANN] ***TRUMP COIN*** THE WINNING COIN***LETS MAKE TRUMP COIN GREAT". A cryptocurrency had been designed to appeal to supporters of Donald J. Trump. The first response to this thread was by user "e1ghtSpace" about eighty eight seconds later. He said:

> "Premine?? No Ninja Launch? Damn. What a shame.
>
> Anyway, lets see how this pans out.
>
> IOS wallet? Well OK this is actually interesting."

FEBRUARY 2016

On the 17th of February at 06:37:23 UTC, user "chicken65" responded to somebody who doubted his integrity and trustworthiness. He was quoted as saying:

> "So, like Trump and in the interests of transparency I tell the truth:
>
> You're wrong that's for a completely different project. Its for a project a group of us are doing in the summer. Half of the team work in advertising and media, we're not coin creators. That one has to be designed fully from scratch because were putting serious money in to it. I work in the music industry, I don't design, create or code wallets with direct access to exchanges. Its not my thing.
> This coin is nothing like that which should be obvious to you if you had any logic and reason. Where do I mention ICO on this one? There is no ICO on Trump Coin
> You think I'm not expecting people to trawl through my previous posts. LOL dude - Clearly you haven't read The Art Of The Deal!
>
> If I wanted to hide anything I wouldn't be using this account."

At the beginning, the development team decided to put a hard limit on the number of coins to be mined. This was 20 million TRUMP. The developers also chose to create a pre-mine (coins mined before the public launch) of 3.5% (700,000 TRUMP). At least half of this pre-mine was destined towards helping promote the coin. User "chicken65" wanted help from as many people as possible to spread awareness of this new cryptocurrency via websites, social media and promotional campaigns. A coin logo design competition was also planned to take place very soon. Two days remained until the scheduled public launch of the blockchain.

On the 19th of February at 07:09:30 UTC, user "chicken65" announced the time and date of the public launch. If they had not already, community members were advised to get ready for mining:

> "Trump Coin Will Be Released
> Friday 19th February
> 7.00pm Eastern Standard Time
> 12.00 Midnight GMT"

As per the pre-announced decision of when the launch was scheduled, the time was met and surpassed without any news the blockchain had gone live. There was confusion why the 20th of February at 00:00:00 UTC had not been honoured. On the 20th of February at 00:07:15 UTC, user "SockPuppetAccount" comically said the following:

> "Launch is 7 minutes late. Has Trump been stumped?"

On the same day at 00:20:29 UTC, user "chicken65" replied by saying:

> "DELAYED RAN IN TO A FEW ISSUES NOTHING SERIOUS BUT WE DONT WANT TO TAKE THE CHANCE BY RUSHING THE RELEASE AND SOMETHING GOING WRONG. HOPE TO HAVE IT DONE IN A FEW HOURS WILL LET YOU KNOW ASAP"

Furthermore, user "chicken65" promised to let the community know within the next couple of hours if the launch was still possible that night (UTC). If yes, there would be a thirty minute warning. If not, it would have to be postponed until the 21st of February 2016. At 02:40:36 UTC, he was quoted as saying:

> "TRUMP COIN ANNOUNCEMENT:
>
> Officially delayed until tomorrow
>
> Much apologies for this but its The best decision to make right now. I have to be 100% sure everything is working. I will not tarnish the Trump with hasty decisions to please a handful of fud artists.
>
> I will announce the release time well ahead of schedule so please keep an eye on the thread.
>
> Again apologies for the inconvenience to you guys who were standing by ready to mine."

FEBRUARY 2016

On the 20th of February at 15:22:06 UTC, user "CryptoSiD" said:

> "www.suchpool.pw/trump ready for launch, pre-reg for now"

This was the first mining pool to publicly announce support for the coin. User "chicken65" was grateful for their support and notified them that the public launch of the blockchain was scheduled to take place at 19:00 EST (or 00:00 UTC on the 21st of February). On the same day at 22:12:02 UTC, user "chicken65" said:

> "Light Block Explorer http://173.44.41.235/index.php
>
> Just under 2 hours until launch"

This time, the public launch of TrumpCoin was successful. However, there was a slight delay in mining at www.suchpool.pw/ due to technical reasons. A tweet was posted shortly after the public launch:

There were immediate calls from members on the official TrumpCoin Bitcointalk thread to initiate trading of the coin on an exchange. YoBit was being considered by user "chicken65" as a realistic and viable option. He was willing to contact them in the next couple of days after the presentational graphics of the coin had been upgraded. A more professional image of the coin was being sought after.

On the 21st of February, the coin's full time programmer called user "TrumpTechGuy" was in the process of adding new features such as mobile wallet apps. Nevertheless, user "chicken65" wanted more focus on the public relations side of the coin, instead of massively devoting time towards the code. As was the case from the beginning, full transparency was promised by user "chicken65".

On the 25th of February, the coin logo design competition began. User "chicken65" was looking for a design which would imitate the appearance of the official website at http://trumpcoin.rocks (still in a preliminary stage). A subtle, classy and smart coin logo was required without it being too overwhelming. A first prize of 10,000 TRUMP (+ 0.1 BTC) stood as an incentive. Second and third position prizes also existed of 6,500 TRUMP and 3,500 TRUMP respectively. Over the next few days, some of the most popular coin logo designs were:

user "DecentralizeEconomics" (both above) user "Panadacoin" user "x100algo"

user "logocreator" (four logo designs above)

FEBRUARY 2016

On the 26th of February, user "chicken65" was disappointed that he had not heard back from YoBit for the last four days. One of the most recent messages sent to the exchange was as follows:

> "ATT YOBIT REP:
>
> I paid the Premium - 0.1 btc - 2 business day for Trump Coin to be listed on your exchange on Monday 22nd. I have repeatedly sent tickets and sent you two personal PM's as well as Tweet YOBIT. I have had Zero response from anyone @ Yobit or your self. You have been online since I sent you those PM's. I understand your busy but I chose the paid service for guaranteed inclusion on your exchange. Please address this situation because I dont think it does YOBIT image any favours."

Notwithstanding the efforts being made to get TRUMP added to YoBit, YoBit was in fact not the first exchange to initiate trading of the coin. An exchange called Vixtrade was the first to add TRUMP at https://vixtrade.net/market/23 on the 28th of February (no longer active).

At a later time on that same day, user "YoBit" announced the following:

> "TrumpCoin [TRUMP] is listed: https://yobit.net/en/trade/TRUMP/BTC
> TrumpCoin Dice: https://yobit.net/en/dice/TRUMP
> Donate TRUMP coins to our Giveaway: https://yobit.net/en/freecoins/
> Please report about TRUMP update/fork/issue here: https://yobit.net/en/reportupdate/TRUMP"

This cryptocurrency exchange went live on the 5th of January 2015.

On the 28th of February at 16:45:11 UTC, user "chicken65" officially announced:

In addition, another graphic of the new logo was unveiled (see page 46).

On the last day of the month, the opening post of the original TrumpCoin Bitcointalk thread was updated to make it look more visually appealing and professional. Reference was also made to the Bitcoin Satoshi value of one unit of TRUMP account (1 BTC Satoshi = 0.00000001 BTC). A value of approximately 250 Bitcoin Satoshi was evident on the YoBit Cryptocurrency Exchange.

Other events which occurred during the month of February were:

- On the 17th of February, http://twitter.com/trumpcoin1 was created.
- On the 21st of February, user "louiseth1" suggested the slogan "Let's Make Crypto Great Again" be adopted by the coin. User "chicken65" concurred.
- On the 27th of February, TrumpCoin was added to the paper wallet generator website at http://anoona-paperwallet.pe.hu/

FEBRUARY 2016

GOP PRIMARY/CAUCUS RESULTS

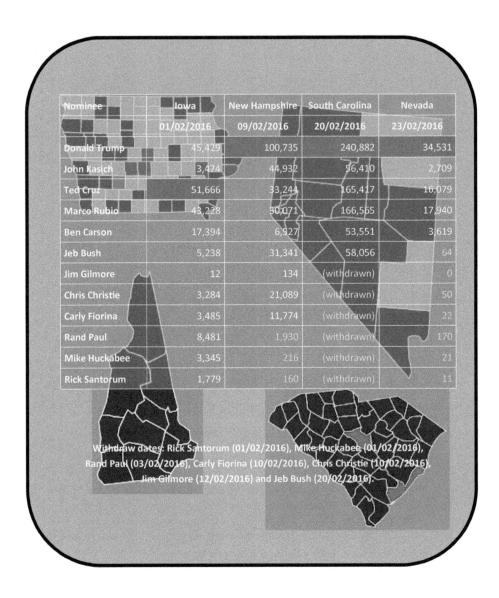

Nominee	Iowa 01/02/2016	New Hampshire 09/02/2016	South Carolina 20/02/2016	Nevada 23/02/2016
Donald Trump	45,429	100,735	240,882	34,531
John Kasich	3,474	44,932	56,410	2,709
Ted Cruz	51,666	33,244	165,417	16,079
Marco Rubio	43,228	30,071	166,565	17,940
Ben Carson	17,394	6,527	53,551	3,619
Jeb Bush	5,238	31,341	58,056	64
Jim Gilmore	12	134	(withdrawn)	0
Chris Christie	3,284	21,089	(withdrawn)	50
Carly Fiorina	3,485	11,774	(withdrawn)	22
Rand Paul	8,481	1,930	(withdrawn)	170
Mike Huckabee	3,345	216	(withdrawn)	21
Rick Santorum	1,779	160	(withdrawn)	11

Withdraw dates: Rick Santorum (01/02/2016), Mike Huckabee (01/02/2016), Rand Paul (03/02/2016), Carly Fiorina (10/02/2016), Chris Christie (10/02/2016), Jim Gilmore (12/02/2016) and Jeb Bush (20/02/2016).

FEBRUARY 2016

VENUES OF TRUMP'S SPEECHES

01/02	Rally	Waterloo, IA
01/02	Rally	Cedar Rapids, IA
02/02	Rally	Milford, NH
03/02	Rally	Little Rock, AR
04/02	Town Hall	Exeter, NH
04/02	Rally	Portsmouth, NH
05/02	Rally	Florence, SC
07/02	Rally	Plymouth, NH
08/02	Town Hall	Salem, NH
08/02	Town Hall	Londonderry, NH
08/02	Rally	Manchester, NH
10/02	Rally	Clemson, SC
11/02	Rally	Baton Rouge, LA
12/02	Rally	Tampa, FL
15/02	Event	Mount Pleasant, SC
15/02	Press Conf	Charleston, SC
15/02	Rally	Greenville, SC
16/02	Rally	North Augusta, SC
16/02	Town Hall	Beaufort, SC
17/02	Town Hall	Bluffton, SC
17/02	Rally	Walterboro, SC
17/02	Rally	Sumter, SC
18/02	Rally	Kiawah, SC
18/02	Event	Gaffney, SC
19/02	Rally	Myrtle Beach, SC
19/02	Town Hall	Pawley's Island, SC
19/02	Rally	Charleston, SC
21/02	Rally	Atlanta, GA
22/02	Rally	Las Vegas, NV
23/02	Rally	Sparks, NV
24/02	Event	Virginia Beach, VA
26/02	Rally	Fort Worth, TX
26/02	Rally	Oklahoma City, OK
27/02	Rally	Bentonville, AR
28/02	Rally	Madison, AL
29/02	Rally	Radford, VA

TrumpCoin—Make Crypto Great Again

FOUNDER CONSIDERED LEAVING TRUMPCOIN AS THE VALUE OF THE COIN SLID

MARCH 2016

I. TrumpCoin added to the website www.coinmarketcap.com.

II. Trump Fund handed over to user "indiemax".

III. Third cryptocurrency exchange called Safecex initiated TRUMP trading.

IV. User "chicken65" contemplated abandoning the coin.

V. Proof of Stake blockchain implementation promised during April.

On the second day of the month, user "chicken65" publicly congratulated Donald J. Trump, his campaign and all his supporters for the gains during "Super Tuesday" on the 1st of March 2016. Donald J. Trump had won seven out of the total eleven primaries/caucuses that night (see page 57 for the results). Also on the 2nd of March at 14:16:25 UTC, user "ozgr" posted the following:

> "Vixtrade.net scam?! 🫠 Withdraw
> Sorry. We do not have enough funds in our hot wallet. Please withdraw later!"

User "chicken65" decided to remove the exchange from the list of recognised exchanges and advised users to discontinue trading there. He said he would contact them to find out what had happened. No response was ever received back.

MARCH 2016

On the 2nd of March at 19:46:20 UTC, user "chicken65" said the following:

> "DEV REQUEST
>
> Does anyone know a highly trusted member who could hold the TRUMP FUND - 450k coins. Def want to keep this whole thing transparent.
> I thought I would ask on the thread here before posting an add. There is one member here who could do it but hes having computer issues
> so doesnt feel confident holding them. They wont be given out to anyone though. Will have to be very trustworthy member. Deal is I send the
> coins to them - they show image - address of coins etc. Of course will have to get rich list sorted out. The person would have to be post publicly of
> course for transparency."

A few minutes after the request, user "Panadacoin" suggested user "SebastianJu" as a very trustworthy escrow service on Bitcointalk. There was a chance he may charge some sort of fee. User "chicken65" responded by saying he viewed him as more of a long term holding service. Instead, he wanted someone who could be called upon to send out coins quickly without a charge each time. User "chicken65" was happy to contact him, but, if it turned out to be more hassle than worthwhile, he would just keep the coins himself until he had found someone else.

On the 4th of March, user "chicken65" made the community aware that any effective public relations of the coin would not go ahead until the value of the coin had stabilised. Also on the 4th of March, new updated Windows and Mac OSX wallet clients were uploaded for users to download. User "chicken65" made users aware of this at 19:59:16 UTC.

On the 5th of March at 08:24:13 UTC, user "Belogvardeec" asked:

> "How many coins already mined?"

A swift response was posted by user "chicken65". A total of approximately 3.2 million TRUMP had been mined to date. However, a new figure of the overall pre-mine was disclosed. Instead of 700,000 TRUMP, a pre-mine of 1 million TRUMP stood. To be exact, 450,000 TRUMP (10% donated) were being held in the Trump Fund, 250,000 by user "chicken65" and another 250,000 by user "TrumpTechGuy".

On the same day at 16:04:53 UTC, user "chicken65" announced the following:

> "DEV ANNOUNCEMENT
>
> We're about to make some changes to the coin which are currently being tested:
>
> Block rewards will be changed from 250 to 100
> Block time will be changed from 120 to 300 seconds
> Coin maturity changed from 100 blocks to 300
> Within a couple of days of these changes POS will be also implemented"

This announcement (later known as just a proposal) was put forward as a response to fight back against some miners who were simply mining and then immediately selling the coin. The developers knew something had to be done about this at some point. The above changes were only tentative. User "TrumpTechGuy" was in the process of testing out various parameters.

On the 7th of March at 13:03:41 UTC, after numerous private messages back and forth between users "chicken65" and "indiemax", user "indiemax" acknowledged that he had just received the Trump Fund. He assured the community it would be kept securely in the wallet address TQE62DG4A9TVBXyM1D83aLA2kZWyVwcn7V.

MARCH 2016

On the previous day, the third exchange initiated direct trading of TRUMP against BTC. On this day at 23:38:48 UTC, user "chicken65" said:

> "DEV ANNOUNCEMENT
> Trump Coin added to SAFECEX EXCHANGE
> https://safecex.com/market?q=TRUMP/BTC"

This exchange is no longer operational. The following was tweeted on the official Safecex Twitter account:

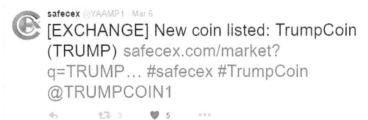

A question was asked whether the TrumpCoin Development Team had contacted Bittrex (a more popular cryptocurrency exchange). On the 7th of March at 19:01:17 UTC, user "chicken65" said:

> "Ive had a very quick conversation with one of their reps. To be blunt, we need to see more trading volume before I can seriously approach them which I totally understand. It will happen at some point Im sure. Also contacted Kraken and its a similar situation. YOBIT is fine for now, but adding another exchange or two will become a priority soon."

On the following day, a discussion was still taking place about whether or not the timestamping algorithm should change to hybrid PoW/PoS or solely PoS at a later date. User "TrumpTechGuy" notified the community of an upcoming hard fork on the 11th of March at 12:00 EST or 17:00 UTC. A new wallet client was scheduled to be available one day beforehand.

MARCH 2016

On the 9th of March, members of the community were encouraged to discuss the potential hard fork of the blockchain. User "chicken65" wanted to know if they wanted it to happen or not. He wanted as much engagement as possible.

On the same day at 19:20:34 UTC, user "chicken65" said:

> "ANNOUNCEMENT REGARDING THE PROPOSED FORK
>
> I've decided to leave the mining specs as they are for now. As a trader I'm more in tune with that type of thinking and my concern has been distribution of the coin. I'll say this though. If some of the miners continue to dump the moment the price rises you do yourself, the coin, and no one else any favours. If you must sell, do it a little at a time. Specs will remain as they are and be reviewed at the end of the month."

Six days later at 23:04:29 UTC, user "chicken65" posted the following:

> "IMPORTANT ANNOUNCEMENT: TRUMPCOIN IS BEING FORKED AT BLOCK 16250"

Shortly after this announcement, the relevant wallet client updates were made available for download and installation. The exchange YoBit temporarily disabled active trading of TRUMP until the hard fork block number had been surpassed. Also on the 15th of March, the total number of TRUMP mined surpassed 5 million. This hard fork went against the announcement.

From block number 16,250, the number of TRUMP rewarded per block to miners was set at 50 TRUMP, instead of 250 TRUMP.

On the 17th of March at 17:25:25 UTC, user "YoBit" said:

> "TrumpCoin market enabled: https://yobit.net/en/trade/TRUMP/BTC"

MARCH 2016

On the 19th of March, user "chicken65" released another announcement in which he was considering to abandon TrumpCoin. He felt pessimistic that someone or a group of people (described as serial dumpers) had simply been selling their mined coins, instead of holding. A low of 80 Bitcoin Satoshi (1 BTC Satoshi equates to 0.00000001 BTC) had been reached. Any development updates (of which there were a few) were postponed until there was clarity that selling had subsided. User "chicken65" said he would make a final personal decision by the 21st of March.

Despite the persistently low Bitcoin Satoshi values of one unit of TRUMP account throughout the month, there was a small recovery on the 20th of March. According to historical values from the cryptocurrency exchange YoBit, these were:

	Price	Low	Open	Close	High	Volume (BTC)
2nd March	941.5	133	583	1,300	2,000	4.30993
5th March	880	350	1,300	460	1,743	6.49265
7th March	486.5	451	460	513	785	4.20508
9th March	508	501	513	503	722	3.75102
11th March	426.5	192	503	350	511	3.51739
13th March	288.5	191	350	227	432	1.34106
16th March	262.5	167	227	298	330	1.13839
18th March	264	229	298	230	300	0.12102
20th March	262.5	80	230	295	295	1.08029

source: https://yobit.net/en/trade/TRUMP/BTC

On the 20th of March, user "chicken65" was relieved to witness selling subside slightly. There were signs, with the support from the community as a whole, that he was starting to feel better about the future prospects of the coin.

MARCH 2016

On the 24th of March at 02:45:06 UTC, user "chicken65" said:

> "Just wanted to say to all that I'm here for the long haul. This dev isn't going to abandon this coin, and this dev has NOT and never will dump on this coin.
>
> I also appreciate tremendously all supporters patience. You will be rewarded for that."

Due to personal circumstances, pressure was building on user "TrumpTechGuy" to get all planned development completed on time. There was hope he would get the "richlist" (a descending list of the richest wallet addresses) released by the 26th of March. User "kprell40" was also setting up a chatroom in which "real time" conversations about coin related material could take place.

On the 25th of March, user "chicken65" noticed that TrumpCoin had recently been added to the mobile wallet application at http://uberpay.io. Two screenshots were:

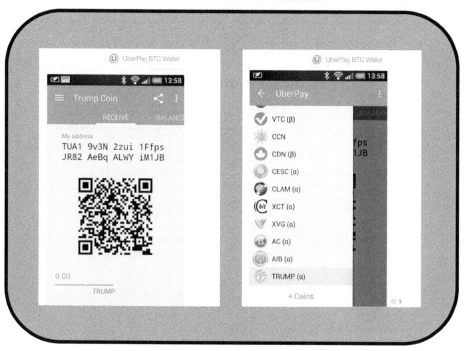

53

MARCH 2016

Users "indiemax", "Signal7", "chicken65" and others were happy to see the recent increase in community participation. Trading volume on YoBit was also increasing. On the 27th of March, the TRUMP/BTC 24 hour trading volume on YoBit peaked at 6.72561 BTC (highest value since the exchange initiated trading of TrumpCoin).

On the 29th of March at 02:02:13 UTC, user "CantStump" was quoted as saying:

> "Great news TRUMP fans:
>
> Looks like Coinmarketcap now has an updated link to the Explorer on the Trumpcoin page: https://coinmarketcap.com/currencies/trumpcoin/
>
> Market Cap and Available Supply are now appearing on Coinmarketcap as well.
>
> This is great stuff!
>
> Thanks to everyone doing their part to help make TRUMP a success!!!"

According to historical data on www.coinmarketcap.com, an approximate market capitalisation of $15,000 was evident. To be exact, a market capitalisation and Bitcoin Satoshi per unit of TRUMP account were $13,773 and 592 respectively.

On the 30th of March at 13:55:27 UTC, user "chicken65" said:

> "Signal Seven and my self have been giving some serious thought to Trump Coin joining up with Microsofts Azure Cloud Network. Just wanted to put the idea out there to see what some of you folks think. Few coins have done this, and it seems Microsoft are begging for coin developers to get in on the act. There are benefits to doing this, valuation of the coin one of them, and the fact that few coins have done this. Maybe Signal could step up with more of the technical details.
>
> https://azure.microsoft.com/en-us/blog/ethereum-blockchain-as-a-service-now-on-azure/"

At the end of the month, user "chicken65" said that TrumpCoin would shift towards a purely proof of stake timestamping algorithm. This would go ahead in about ten days.

On the 30th of March at 14:30:17 UTC, user "CoinHopper" was quoted as saying:

> "Can anyone give me 2 reasons why this coin will be worth more later in life then it is today. Im just looking for 2 real good reasons.."

User "Signal7" responded by saying:

> "Here. Have 10.
>
> 1. Dedicated and active dev team who are actually honest, helpful and hell-bent on creating an environment of profitable and stable fair trade.
> 2. A proven track record of price swings that correlate with political events.
> 3. A name and motto that has wide recognition. Like it or hate it, you have an opinion.
> 4. POW is almost over. POS is coming in about 10 days.
> 5. Eth integration coming with smart contracts for easy exchange, fun games, loans, crowdsales, crowdfunding, arbitration automation, liens, merge mining, and more.
> 6. Azure integration coming within 10 days (EXPOSURE).
> 7. Online wallets (almost finished).
> 8. Becoming increasingly scarce with every move we make.
> 9. Social-political rally coming this summer with a "Make money great again!" theme to ride the coat tails of the times.
> 10. The hidden roadmap that builds off of this preamble (Shit. I said too much)."

User "chicken65" stated that his motivation and dedication towards TrumpCoin had never been stronger. Spurred on by support from the community, he was keen to further promote the "free society" message of the coin to a wider audience of people. He viewed Twitter as the best way to achieve this.

Efforts were still being made to get the coin on further exchanges.

MARCH 2016

Other events which occurred in the month of March were:

- On the 11th of March, user "indiemax" encouraged community members to donate towards the Trump Fund at the TrumpCoin wallet address TQE62DG4A9TVBXyM1D83aLA2kZWyVwcn7V. Consequently, user "nid125", "Depredation", "Signal7" and "chicken65" sent 5,125, 1,941, 1,000 and 5,000 TRUMP respectively. User "chicken65" said the fund would be used wisely.
- An online wallet was made accessible at http://trumpcoin.rocks/wallet/ on the 12th of March. People were politely asked to test it and report any issues. Also on this day, user "Signal7" released a mining cost/profit calculator.
- On the 25th of March, user "CantStump" founded an IRC Channel at #trumpcoin on the server irc.rizon.net. He welcomed all those who wanted to participate in a lively conversation. Skype and Zello were also mentioned by user "chicken65" as viable discussion mediums.
- On the 26th of March, user "rainzxyz" added a block explorer for TrumpCoin at http://www.rainz.xyz/chainz/trump/. On the following day, he was pleased to announce that TrumpCoin had been added to the complementary faucet at http://www.rainz.xyz/rainz/trump/.

MARCH 2016

GOP PRIMARY/CAUCUS RESULTS

		Donald Trump	John Kasich	Ted Cruz	Marco Rubio	Ben Carson
AL	01/03	373,721	38,199	181,479	160,606	88,094
AK	01/03	7,740	918	8,369	3,488	2,492
AR	01/03	134,744	15,305	125,340	101,910	23,521
GA	01/03	502,994	72,508	305,847	316,836	80,723
MA	01/03	312,425	114,434	60,592	113,170	16,360
MN	01/03	24,473	6,565	33,181	41,397	8,422
OK	01/03	130,267	16,524	158,078	119,633	28,601
TN	01/03	333,180	45,301	211,471	181,274	64,951
TX	01/03	758,762	120,473	1,241,118	503,055	117,969
VT	01/03	19,974	18,534	5,932	11,781	2,551
VA	01/03	356,840	97,784	171,150	327,918	60,228
KS	05/03	18,443	8,741	37,512	13,295	582
KY	05/03	82,493	33,134	72,503	37,579	1,951
LA	05/03	124,854	19,359	113,968	33,813	4,544
ME	05/03	6,070	2,270	8,550	1,492	132
PR	06/03	5,474	582	3,610	28,937	168

On the 4th of March, Ben Carson withdrew from the race to become the Republican Nominee for US President. Seven days later, he officially endorsed Donald J. Trump.

MARCH 2016

GOP PRIMARY/CAUCUS RESULTS

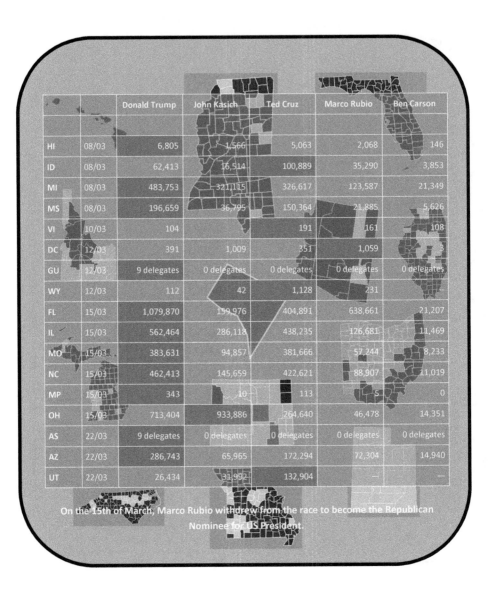

		Donald Trump	John Kasich	Ted Cruz	Marco Rubio	Ben Carson
HI	08/03	6,805	1,566	5,063	2,068	146
ID	08/03	62,413	16,514	100,889	35,290	3,853
MI	08/03	483,753	321,115	326,617	123,587	21,349
MS	08/03	196,659	36,795	150,364	21,885	5,626
VI	10/03	104		191	161	108
DC	12/03	391	1,009	351	1,059	
GU	12/03	9 delegates	0 delegates	0 delegates	0 delegates	0 delegates
WY	12/03	112	42	1,128	231	
FL	15/03	1,079,870	159,976	404,891	638,661	21,207
IL	15/03	562,464	286,118	438,235	126,681	11,469
MO	15/03	383,631	94,857	381,666	57,244	8,233
NC	15/03	462,413	145,659	422,621	88,907	11,019
MP	15/03	343	10	113	5	0
OH	15/03	713,404	933,886	264,640	46,478	14,351
AS	22/03	9 delegates	0 delegates	0 delegates	0 delegates	0 delegates
AZ	22/03	286,743	65,965	172,294	72,304	14,940
UT	22/03	26,434	31,992	132,904	–	–

On the 15th of March, Marco Rubio withdrew from the race to become the Republican Nominee for US President.

MARCH 2016

VENUES OF TRUMP'S SPEECHES

01/03	Rally	Columbus, OH
01/03	Rally	Louisville, KY
03/03	Rally	Portland, ME
03/03	Rally	Warren, MI
04/03	Rally	Cadillac, MI
04/03	Rally	New Orleans, LA
05/03	Rally	Wichita, KS
05/03	Press Conf	West Palm Beach, FL
05/03	Rally	Orlando, FL
07/03	Rally	Concord, NC
07/03	Rally	Madison, MS
09/03	Rally	Fayetteville, NC
11/03	Rally	St. Louis, MO
11/03	Rally	Chicago, IL
12/03	Rally	Kansas City, MO

12/03	Rally	Dayton, OH
12/03	Rally	Cleveland, OH
13/03	Town Hall	Cincinnati, OH
13/03	Rally	Bloomington, IL
14/03	Town Hall	Tampa, FL
14/03	Town Hall	Hickory, NC
18/03	Rally	Salt Lake City, UT
19/03	Rally	Tucson, AR
21/03	Pres Conf	Old Post Office, DC
21/03	Speech	AIPAC Policy Conf
29/03	Pres Conf	Janesville, WI
29/03	Town Hall	Janesville, WI
30/03	Rally	De Pere, WI
30/03	Rally	Appleton, WI

On the 11th of March, the rally in Chicago, IL was cancelled. Protesters had infiltrated the arena in which Donald J. Trump was going to speak.

TRANSITION TO THE NEW POS BLOCKCHAIN
APRIL 2016

I. First known independent news article published about TrumpCoin.
II. Block number one of the new blockchain was timestamped.
III. C-Cex initiated direct trading between BTC and TRUMP.
IV. One unit of TRUMP account surged in value on the 14th of April.
V. C-Cex initiated direct trading between BTC and USD.

Since the introduction of the coin two months ago, it had been described as a scam, ridiculed and attacked by certain individuals or groups. Nevertheless, the development team were fully committed to further expand and enhance the appeal of TrumpCoin to a wider audience.

One particular question was asked during the first few days of the month. It was "What if Donald J. Trump doesn't become the nominee or president?". User "chicken65" assured the community that TrumpCoin would remain active into the foreseeable future regardless of what was going to happen. Its initial free society message would stay strong. Efforts were still being made to bring TrumpCoin to the attention of prominent members of Trump's campaign team and followers.

A very important announcement was going to be made about the coin's future in the next few days. The developers were keen to sustain the longevity of the coin.

APRIL 2016

On the 6th of April at 16:26 EST, the first known independent news article specifically about TrumpCoin was published at http://vocativ.com. Written by Kevin Collier, it was titled "Introducing TrumpCoin, The Currency For Fans Of Donald Trump". There were users on Bitcointalk who thought this was great exposure for TrumpCoin. At the time, Vocativ were registering about five million page views per month and comfortably resided in the top 20,000 websites worldwide. Journalist Kevin Collier had contacted user "chicken65" via Skype. The full article can be read in the appendix of this book on pages 137 to 139.

vocativ

On the same day at 17:11:23 UTC, user "chicken65" posted the awaited announcement about Trumpcoin shifting to a brand new blockchain (V2 Blockchain to be launched publicly on the 14th of April 2016). He was quoted as saying:

> "After two months in existence Trump Coin is about to make a big and positive change for its investors and its future. At the moment Trump Coin is slightly hampered by its limited possibilities in terms of embracing Tech (particularly cutting edge Tech) and usability across the spectrum of the digital ecosphere. What's being built in to the V2 coin will mean an exciting and open future which will embrace and implement the latest cutting edge Tech whilst at the same time maintaining it core belief of a Free Society message and wider adoption possibilities."

A description of how the transition from the old to the new blockchain was subsequently given. An opportunity would arise to allow users to swap (1 for 1) their old coins (V1) for new coins (V2) via a user friendly website. All the swaps would be done manually, anonymity respected and an e-mail required for verification purposes. The plan was to begin the swap on the 11th of April. User "chicken65" advised members of the community to keep informed by regularly referring to the official TrumpCoin Bitcointalk thread.

Sometime in the next week, the development team wanted to professionally begin contacting main stream media (MSM) outlets.

APRIL 2016

On the 8th of April at 15:19:51 UTC, user "chicken65" said:

> "TRUMP V2 COIN SWAP REMINDER
>
> We will be testing the coin swap over the weekend and from Monday you should be able to swap. Keep an eye on the thread for information."

In the early hours (UTC) of the 9th of April, the Bitcoin Satoshi value of one unit of TRUMP account surpassed 2,000 for the first time. According to the US Dollar value of one Bitcoin ($416.933) on the website www.bitinfocharts.com, this equated to roughly $0.00833866 per TRUMP.

On the 10th of April, voting to get the coin added to the exchange C-Cex began at https://c-cex.com/?id=vote. It reached number one spot on this list one day later.

On the following day at 01:48:21 UTC, user "Signal7" was quoted as saying:

> "A Very Special Announcement
>
> Trumpcoin V2 has given birth to a beautiful and healthy new genesis block at 1460334137 unix time.
>
> Testing has completed and the new production chain is now live. We are on schedule to release the new wallet tomorrow and begin the swap."

On the 11th of April at 03:43:59 UTC, the community were made aware that the swap was not live yet. The development team said full instructions would be available as soon as everything else was ready to go. The swap would be open for several days to give people ample time to participate.

Following on from the genesis block, block number one was timestamped:

Block #1 (Reward 6,500,000 TRUMP) April 11th 2016 at 11:01:32 AM UTC

APRIL 2016

Despite information about the swap being present on the official Trumpcoin Bitcointalk thread, there were people who were confused. User "chicken65" reiterated public launch on the 14th of April, and promised to give an exact time before this. A tentative time of 20:00 EST was given. User "chicken65" unveiled the URL where users could later (to be announced) swap their coins:

> http://trumpcoin.rocks/swap/forms/trumpcoin-v1-to-v2-swap/0

Some users asked why the swap could not be done automatically by YoBit. This was dismissed as impractical due to lacklustre communication with this exchange. If any users were late swapping, user "chicken65" was prepared to allow a few days before the V1 blockchain finally ceased to operate. Instructions on how to use the above swap site and the wallet client updates were going to be posted later. Also, testing of the new blockchain had been successful over the weekend. User "chicken65" encouraged anyone with questions to get in contact straight away.

On the 12th of April at 20:44:26 UTC, user "chicken65" announced the following:

> "Trump Coin is now on CCEX. This is your current Trump Coin, not the V2 so trade as normal.
>
> We had to be a little sneaky here for a number of reasons I dont need to go in to. Thanks to Signal7 who helped enormously with this part of the development.
>
> I would like to also take this oppurtunity to recommend trading at CCEX over YOBIT. However that is your choice.
>
> Swapping to V2 will still commence as normal. However you will be able to do this directly via CCEX, but not yobit. You will also still be able to swap manually if you wish. We wanted all angles covered. This will hopefully put an end to the aggressive anti Trump individuals on the thread who clearly had vested interests which had nothing to do with them trading this coin or being part of the community.
>
> https://c-cex.com/?p=trmp1-btc"

APRIL 2016

In the late hours (UTC) of the 12th of April, new wallet clients (both Windows and Mac OS X) were made available for download. There were also three ways by which users would be able to swap their old TRUMP for new TRUMP. These were:

1. All V1 TRUMP on C-Cex (not YoBit) will automatically swap to V2 TRUMP.
2. One can do it manually via the swap site (full instructions tomorrow).
3. Send V1 TRUMP to user "chicken65" who will then send back V2 TRUMP.

On the 13th of April at 02:26:44 UTC, user "Signal7" said:

> "C-CEX was a pleasure to deal with to set everything up. Support has been very responsive and helpful. I am impressed by how professional everyone has been.
> I have been enjoying trading there since the upgrades. Some of the tools are pretty cool and the atmosphere is way more chill. I feel very good about C-CEX doing the swap."

As promised, full instructions on how to use the swap website were published before the swap went live.

On the 14th of April at 01:21:07 UTC, user "chicken65" said:

> "Just wanted to emphasise this. Whilst you will not be able to trade with V2 Trumps until Friday you can swap your V1 Trumps for V2 Trumps tomorrow via the swap site option
>
> You can start swapping your coins after 6.00pm GMT - 1.00pm EST. You will not be able to trade your V2 coins until CCEX has swapped to V2 Trumps on the exchange on Friday. Of course you can leave your Trump V1 coins in CCEX exchange and they will be automatically swapped to Trump V2's.
>
> This is by far the easiest method. You dont have to do a thing.
>
> ill also take this opportunity to mention the ann will be re designed as will the website and ready for the official launch of Trump V2 on Friday."

APRIL 2016

On the 14th of April at 15:08:32 UTC, user "chicken65" said:

> "If anyone wishes to start transferring their coins via the swap site now they can do so now.
>
> I know I'm ahead of schedule but some have already started doing it so I may as well go along with it.
>
> PLEASE read the instructions on the (large) transfer instruction post I made above or at the beginning of the Ann. I will repost it a number of times."

Daily trading volume, the Bitcoin Satoshi value of one unit of TRUMP account and the market capitalisation reached all time highs on the 14th of April. This peak in market capitalisation would eventually be surpassed on the 29th of June. As can be seen below, these were:

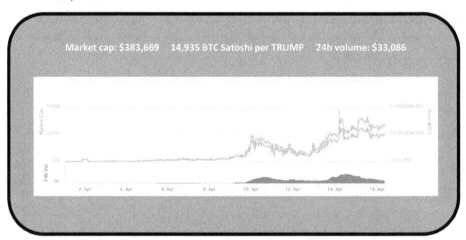

Taking into account that the average US Dollar value of Bitcoin was $424.55 on this day, one unit of TRUMP account was approximately $0.0634.

In the very late hours of the 14th of April, the new redesign of the official TrumpCoin website was unveiled and went live. It was still located at the same domain address http://trumpcoin.rocks.

On the 15th of April at 13:00 UTC, the new blockchain publicly launched. User "TechTrumpGuy" was quick to point out that the network protocol had been designed to accept proof of work blocks for the first 10,000 blocks after which all blocks will be proof of stake. Proof of work had been used to make sure the blockchain sustained staking for that period. The block reward generated during proof of work was zero, except for the 6.5 million at block number one.

On the 15th of April at 12:20:50 UTC, user "Signal7" said:

> "To all exchanges and pools:
>
> Effective Immediately
> Version 1 of Trumpcoin (TRUMP) is longer supported since 8:00 AM EST, Friday, April 15, 2016.
>
> Users are currently swapping the coin externally to a new chain. You are welcome to swap your clients and continue listing the new V2 coin. Please install the new node and swap your users or begin the delisting process for TRUMP at your earliest convenience.
>
> The new GIT can be downloaded from
> https://github.com/TRUMPCOIN/V2TRUMP
>
> All other listed information for TRUMP remains unchanged at this time.
>
> Thank you, Trumpcoin"

In the late hours of the 15th of April, users were enquiring whether the coins on YoBit were V1 or V2. User "chicken65" said they were still using the V1 blockchain and he had been trying to convince them to swap or delist TRUMP entirely.

On the following day, YoBit ceased TrumpCoin deposits and withdraws. At the end of that day, they had transitioned to the new blockchain and, as a result, trading was again possible.

Instead of a hard global cap of 20 million TRUMP, the cap was now 12 million. A different hashing algorithm was operational (Blake-256). Staking coins in one's wallet client would result in the chance of that user gaining 2% annually.

APRIL 2016

Another exchange (viewed as minor) was called Novaexchange. It is unknown when they initiated trading of TrumpCoin, but user "Signal7" on the 18th of April at 13:57:28 UTC confirmed that they had transitioned to the new V2 blockchain. He had personally assisted the exchange in this process.

Voting to get the coin on other popular cryptocurrency exchanges such as Poloniex and Bittrex became more evident as the month progressed. Eager members of the community were submitting their reviews to https://poloniex.com/coinRequest.

On the 21st of April at 18:07:38 UTC, user "Signal7" said:

> "www.MakeMoneyGreatAgain.org
>
> The framework is up now and the first landing page is online.
>
> I'm still testing through some things and wrapping up some of the content but I thought you all might enjoy another teaser."

During the next few days, there were hardly any news or updates. Work was happening behind the scenes to make TrumpCoin a great success.

On the 25th of April at 17:59:44 UTC, user "chicken65" said:

> "http://makemoneygreatagain.org/Content/Guides/Guides.aspx
>
> We (signal7) has created the beginnings of a site aimed at newcomers. This site and its features will eventually expand but hopefully it gives an idea as to where were going and our intentions.
> There was a reason for the V2 switch, the inclusion of the Tech - Tether coming up etc. Its not made up nonsense to try and sell a few coins. The V1 coin was not suitable for the Trump name.
> He doesnt build low quality and neither do we. Im also personally doing something in the background that could be very exciting if I pull it off."

As the month came to a close, a discussion ensued about the number of users who were trolling the official TrumpCoin Bitcointalk thread. User "chicken65" proposed whether creating a new moderated thread could reduce the "fud".

Bitcoin Satoshi values of one unit of TRUMP account on both YoBit (YB) and C-Cex (CC) had gradually fallen. Values during the last four days of April were:

	Price	Low	Open	Close	High	Volume (TRUMP)
27th April (YB)	3,975.5	2,606	5,175	2,776	5,250	106,677.12
27th April (CC)	4,501	3,010	4,002	5,000	6,845	89,965.73
28th April (YB)	4,164.5	2,801	4,550	3,779	4,700	21,389.56
28th April (CC)	4,225.5	3,100	5,000	3,451	5,000	36,020.80
29th April (YB)	3,589	1,501	3,779	3,399	3,799	272,941.23
29th April (CC)	2,826	1,950	3,451	2,201	3,573	52,900.18
30th April (YB)	2,650	1,687	3,399	1,901	3,399	126,295.02
30th April (CC)	2,914.5	1,602	3,285	2,544	3,290	70,403.01

source: www.cryptocompare.com

Other events which occurred in the month of April were:

- On the 13th of April, the subreddit at https://reddit.com/r/trumpcoin was created. The number of posts there has been low.

- On the 14th of April at 21:27:15 UTC, user "indiemax" notified the community that the Trump Fund had been swapped from V1 to V2.

- On the 15th of April, user "chicken65" was looking for someone to administer a TrumpCoin Facebook Community Page. This never happened.

- A TRUMP/USD market opened at https://c-cex.com/?p=trump-usd on the 17th of April.

APRIL 2016

GOP PRIMARY/CAUCUS RESULTS

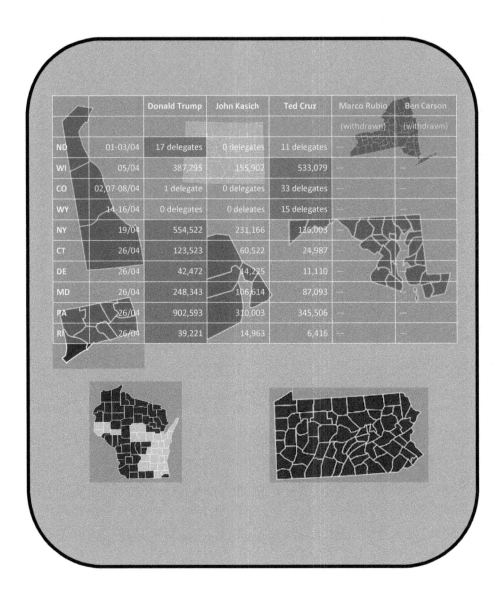

		Donald Trump	John Kasich	Ted Cruz	Marco Rubio (withdrawn)	Ben Carson (withdrawn)
ND	01-03/04	17 delegates	0 delegates	11 delegates	—	—
WI	05/04	387,295	155,902	533,079	—	—
CO	02,07-08/04	1 delegate	0 delegates	33 delegates	—	—
WY	14-16/04	0 delegates	0 deleates	15 delegates	—	—
NY	19/04	554,522	231,166	126,003	—	—
CT	26/04	123,523	60,522	24,987	—	—
DE	26/04	42,472	14,225	11,110	—	—
MD	26/04	248,343	106,614	87,093	—	—
PA	26/04	902,593	310,003	345,506	—	—
RI	26/04	39,221	14,963	6,416	—	—

APRIL 2016

VENUES OF TRUMP'S SPEECHES

02/04	Speech	Racine, WI
02/04	Speech	Wausau, WI
02/04	Rally	Eau Claire, WI
03/04	Rally	West Allis, WI
04/04	Rally	La Crosse, WI
04/04	Rally	Superior, WI
04/04	Rally	Milwaukee, WI
06/04	Rally	Bethpage, NY
10/04	Rally	Rochester, NY
11/04	Rally	Albany, NY
12/04	Rally	Rome, NY
13/04	Rally	Pittsburgh, PA
14/04	Speech	Patchogue, NY
14/04	Speech	Republican Gala, NY
15/04	Rally	Plattsburgh, NY
15/04	Rally	Hartford, CT
16/04	Rally	Watertown, NY
17/04	Pres Conf	Staten Island, NY
17/04	Speech	Richmond County, NY
18/04	Rally	Buffalo, NY
20/04	Rally	Indianapolis, IN
20/04	Rally	Ocean City, MD
21/04	Rally	Harrisburg, PA
22/04	Rally	Harrington, DE
23/04	Rally	Waterburg, CT
23/04	Rally	Bridgeport, CT
24/04	Rally	Hagerstown, MD
25/04	Rally	Warwick, RI
25/04	Rally	West Chester, PA
25/04	Rally	Wilkes-Barre, PA
27/04	Speech	Washington, DC
27/04	Rally	Indianapolis, IN
28/04	Rally	Evansville, IN
28/04	Rally	Costa Mesa, CA
29/04	Speech	CAGOP Convention

TrumpCoin—Make Crypto Great Again

TRUMPCOIN PROMOTIONAL VIDEO UPLOADED TO YOUTUBE
MAY 2016

I. Efforts made to get the coin noticed by the official Trump Campaign Team.
II. Silence from the TrumpCoin Development Team.
III. A 20,000 TRUMP bounty offered to create a "How To Consumer Site".
IV. Video "Introducing: TrumpCoin?" uploaded to YouTube.
V. Exchange called Cryptopia LLC initiated live TRUMP/BTC trading.

As a continuation from prior months, the community were still trying to contact well known people involved in Donald J. Trump's campaign team. Two individuals mentioned were "Diamond and Silk" who had been strong supporters of Donald Trump for some time. User "DecentralizeEconomics" suggested that they create a video about TrumpCoin. This never became reality.

On the 1st of May at 09:14:51 UTC, user "chicken65" said:

> "Trump V2 smart coin can utilise the latest tech in Crypto. Its essentially now an ETH building platform ie Dapps etc. We are keen to get moving on this but feel we need to let some people cool off and let the market settle before we start rolling out some new integrations. The reason we went V2 was longevity. As a regular legacy coin there really wasnt much we could do with the coin. V2 opened up the doors to many possibilities."

MAY 2016

On the 4th of May at 16:33:15 UTC, user "chicken65" said:

> "DEV INFO: What we're trying behind the scenes is get the coin to Trumps attention. I have been trying direct by contacting some people on his campaign team or people he is friends with. So far no joy but I will keep trying. Another way is less direct route such as contacting Diamond and Silk. If they were to endorse the coin the word might get back to Trump. So, basically that's what's going on behind the scenes. You can help by directly tweeting Trump, or anyone on his campaign team, or anyone he is friends with. At some point it will be brought to his attention. It is then he decides to sue or not. I'm 100% certain he wouldn't sue. Im not 100% certain of his endorsement, but its something we have to try. Endorsement pushed the Ron Paul coin to $6. I cant see how an endorsement wouldn't do the same for Trump Coin
>
> FYI When I send out the emails to Trumps team I do offer a % of profits from the Trump Fund for any cause Donald Trump wishes."

Throughout the second half of April, the Bitcoin Satoshi value of one unit of TRUMP account had gradually decreased. As can be seen below, the value increased in the first few days of May. Values from YoBit (YB) and C-Cex (CC) were:

	Price	Low	Open	Close	High	Volume (TRUMP)
1st May (YB)	2,239	1,303	1,901	2,577	3,450	223,922.92
1st May (CC)	2,946	1,522	2,544	3,348	3,350	110,225.58
2nd May (YB)	2,555	2,075	2,700	2,410	2,798	140,180.78
2nd May (CC)	3,066.5	1,701	3,348	2,785	3,348	5,311.04
3rd May (YB)	3,180	2,408	2,410	3,950	4,444	387,244.54
3rd May (CC)	2,902.5	1,806	1,806	3,999	3,999	46,046.78
4th May (YB)	4,524.5	3,503	3,950	5,099	5,800	202,434.26
4th May (CC)	4,299.5	2,502	3,999	4,600	6,700	154,708.32

source: www.cryptocompare.com

MAY 2016

For about one week, beginning on the 6th of May, there was silence and no posts made by user "chicken65". Some members of the community were beginning to get agitated and concerned. They wanted to know whether user "chicken65", the Lead Project Manager, had bailed out and abandoned TrumpCoin. Finally, he submitted a post at 23:59:01 UTC on the 13th of May:

> "Apologies for the delay in posting.
>
> Some things have happened that I believe require a bit of a course correction for the project. Its nothing for anyone to worry about, its a positive thing - but neither is it something to get uber excited about. However, if we go this route I believe coin/project will gain much more than it loses. Ill post more information in a day or two, just wanted to give a heads up."

He made the community aware of his other commitments (his small company which had suffered a bit since the launch of Trumpcoin, so he had to catch up on that). He assured everyone he would not be someone to simply vanish. Members of the community were happy to hear an update from him. A few people were starting to get concerned that no news/updates were being made regularly. On the 14th of May at 19:58:01 UTC, user "indiemax" said:

> "Great to see you Dev
>
> The TRUMP can't be STUMPED"

People had also noticed the absence of another member of the community. The last post submitted by user "Signal7" on the official TrumpCoin Bitcointalk thread was on the 26th of April at 19:26:28 UTC. User "chicken65" assumed he had bailed out due to persistent threats from others. User "chicken65" suggested user "Signal7" had "bitten off more than he can chew". Whatever the real reason, lack of communication between people was stoking the fire of rumours. It would not be until the 27th of May at 17:37:09 UTC that user "Signal7" posted again.

MAY 2016

On the 17th of May at 18:44:31 UTC, user "chicken65" voiced his concerns about the lack of active community involvement. He knew he could not do everything. He also had limited time due to running his own business. As a means to move things forward, he created a bounty campaign:

> "Consumer/Trump Supporters guide website - 15,000 Trump Coins to whoever creates a site that shows in detail how the non crypto person can get hold of BTC to purchase Trump Coins. Ive had quite a few emails about how to do this and believe me its hard to explain to a complete newcomer over email .They tend to give up. They need help. So, this site would have some video demos (which I can help with) and text explaining how to buy BTC and convert to Trumps. Also a little info on basic trading.
>
> Keep in mind they can actually transfer dollars directly to CCEX so its not as difficult for them as it first seems. A site like this would be of great help to all of us. Anyone familiar with using wordpress templates will easily be able to do something like this."

Also on the 17th of May, user "chicken65" appreciated the Facebook page user "NewWorldOrder" created four days previously. However, he thought improvements could still be made to its appearance. He wanted user "NewWorldOrder" to contact him.

Two days later, the bounty campaign to create a 'How To Consumer Site' for Trump supporters was increased from 15,000 TRUMP to 20,000 TRUMP.

On the 23rd of May at 16:40:53 UTC, user "chicken65" said:

> "Were about to become a full on Presidential campaign funding project. For Trump supporters it will be spelled out like this.
>
> 'By investing in Trump Coins your helping Donald Trump to become President because by simply buying the coins your effectively increasing the value of the 200k Trump coins for his Presidential campaign. +++ U can also make profit. Its a win situation for all parties
>
> Something like that Website/Ann and Teth should all be complete this week."

MAY 2016

On the 25th of May at 16:09:58 UTC, user "TrumpCoinContent" said:

> https://www.youtube.com/watch?v=iMM-X0mDonI&feature=youtu.be
>
> "Here you go ladies and gents
>
> Above is the "Introducing: TrumpCoin" promotional video, about a minute long and ready to roll out. If there's any changes you want included in the bio or the video itself I'm happy to accommodate.
>
> I'll be 100% honest with you guys, I idiotically bought high when it was pumping about a month ago and missed out on some pretty hefty trumps. I don't expect any number but if you guys are feeling generous I'd love nothing more than to have 100k in Trumps to hold onto and watch grow (the amount I would have got had I timed it better as opposed to the 11k I goofed on ahah). I want to watch this thing reach at least 20$$ a Trump so I have no plans in dumping whatever little I can get my hands on. You're all the best and I'm stoked to be able to contribute in some small way. As well as the video above, I also have some history in generating viral attention and some blog/news coverage, the kind of coverage I think TrumpCoin really needs, so if anyone wants that I can do my best to get the ball rolling.
>
> TLPSDWJfbZmHUf4oGEA4YKpKNN49toypyE (here is my v2 TRUMP wallet, would make my year if you guys could help me moon with y'all in any small way)
>
> If you like the vid would be happy to contribute more, I'm also a designer and run a few marketing pages."

Both users "sethspof" and "NewWorldOrder" donated 200 and 500 TRUMP respectively as a thank you. They also both promised to donate more if the video was able to get over 1,000 views. At the beginning of October, the video had approx. 13,200 views. On the 26th of May at 01:12:04 UTC, user "chicken65" said:

> "Great stuff thanks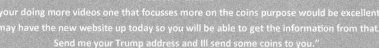
> If your doing more videos one that focusses more on the coins purpose would be excellent. I may have the new website up today so you will be able to get the information from that. Send me your Trump address and Ill send some coins to you."

MAY 2016

This was the first promotional video created for TrumpCoin. What follows is the full transcript of what was said during it:

Donald Trump: "So, they rip us off, they take our money, they make us look like fools, and now they're back to being who they really are. And we're going to get nothing, nothing! We are led by very, very stupid people. We cannot let it continue. We are a country that owes 19 trillion dollars."

Narrator One: "30 years no tax reform, 30 years nothing on immigrations. As a result, you have this movement toward a guy like Donald Trump.

Ron Paul: "Does the Bitcoin fit the mould to be a challenger to the Dollar, a substitute for the Dollar...?"

Narrator 2: "What brought it to my attention is the need for alternatives in our current monetary system.

Narrator 3: "And then, but here, all I can say about what the United States is doing, it is, is, it's immoral!

Donald Trump: "It will change!"

Cenk Uygur: "Oh oh, what's the chance Donald Trump's going to win? Well, according to the polls, by the way are a reality of what Americans are thinking today, the chances are pretty damn good."

Donald Trump: "We are going to make America great again!"

Donald Trump: "We will have so much winning if I get elected that you may get bored with winning."

Oprah Winfrey: "This sounds like political presidential talk to me. I know people have talked to you about whether or not you want to run. Would you, would you ever...?"

Donald Trump: "I would never want to rule it out totally."

On the 26th of May, user "chicken65" hoped to have the newly designed opening post of the original TrumpCoin Bitcointalk thread and official website (www.trumpcoin.rocks) completed. It did not happen. He promised to have it done by the 29th of May. A significant change to the image of the coin was planned to make TrumpCoin a "profit driven presidential campaigning/donation machine".

On the 27th of May at 15:25:09 UTC, user "TrumpCoinContent" said:

> https://www.youtube.com/watch?v=iMM-X0mDonI&feature=youtu.be
>
> "1k views for the Introducing Trumpcoin video y'all...small milestone but a milestone nonetheless
>
> Happy to put out more if needed and can help with marketing viral strategy based on media manipulation where possible
>
> If you'd like any more content please tell me what you're after specifically, what designs and aesthetics you need etc.
>
> TLPSDWJfbZmHUf4oGEA4YKpKNN49toypyE (my trump address if you're so kind as to donate to the TrumpCoinContent Moon Fund)
>
> M A G A
> A
> G
> A"

As promised, user "NewWorldOrder" donated a further 500 TRUMP to user "TrumpCoinContent".

User "Signal7" eventually submitted a post on the official TrumpCoin Bitcointalk thread on the 27th of May at 17:37:09 UTC. He was glad to be back. It was also on this day that he updated the site www.MakeCryptoGreatAgain.org by adding a real-time coin statistics ticker to it. Visitors to that website could, from this point forward, see the US Dollar value of the Trump Fund. In addition, the video created by "TrumpCoinContent" was added to that website.

MAY 2016

On the 28th of May, the sixth cryptocurrency exchange called Cryptopia initiated trading of TRUMP against Bitcoin. Cryptopia Limited (an LLC in New Zealand) announced the addition on their official Twitter page at 07:52 UTC. It is an exchange that has been active since the 6th of December 2014. Their logo is:

Also on the 28th of May at 23:23:27 UTC, the official website at www.trumpcoin.rocks and the original TrumpCoin Bitcointalk thread were announced as fully updated by user "chicken65". The intention was to keep things simple, especially for newcomers. Without the need to understand the underlying programming code of TrumpCoin, people would need assistance to find out how to buy the coin and how it could then be used. The community were still waiting for somebody to produce a "How To Video" describing how one buys TrumpCoin with Bitcoin and the other things besides this.

On the 29th of May at 06:28:34 UTC, user "chicken65" announced the following:

> "I have setup a wallet which holds the Trump Campaign Fund as well as the direct sales fund:
>
> Trump Fund Campaign Donation Address:
> TUH1KDnwVj5ELnsEokrPoSqi2jDKSUsgr9 - 200k Trumps
>
> Trump Direct Sales Fund:
> TNE9aWPKjAbCU6qQtZZ1jWHDzU2c6xfWbt - 100k Trumps
>
> All direct sales income will be used to purchase Trump Coins from the sell orders.
> Any unsold will be added to the Trump Campaign Fund
> If donating make sure you donate to the Trump Fund Campaign Address"

MAY 2016

Other events which occurred in the month of May were:

- Donald J. Trump won the Indiana Primary on the 3rd of May.

- On the 13th of May, user "NewWorldOrder" founded the Facebook group at https://facebook.com/trump.coin.3. User "chicken65" praised him for creating it three days later.

- On the 16th of May, an online Trump Casino using TrumpCoin was proposed by user "Embat". No interest in the proposal was shown.

- Another Facebook group was created on the 19th of May by user "NewWorldOder" at http://facebook.com/TrumpCoinCryptocurrency/. A total of 10,000 TRUMP were subsequently allocated towards funding the Facebook Advertisement Campaign on there.

- On the 20th of May, the National Rifle Association (NRA) endorsed Donald J. Trump for US President. The NRA have over five million members.

- On the 26th of May, the Twitter account https://twitter.com/InvestinTRUMP was created.

- On the 28th of May, user "chicken65" said that he was going to commission an official TrumpCoin video. He described the video uploaded three days ago as great, but wanted one that said what TrumpCoin is and its purpose within the first 15 seconds.

MAY 2016

GOP PRIMARY/CAUCUS RESULTS

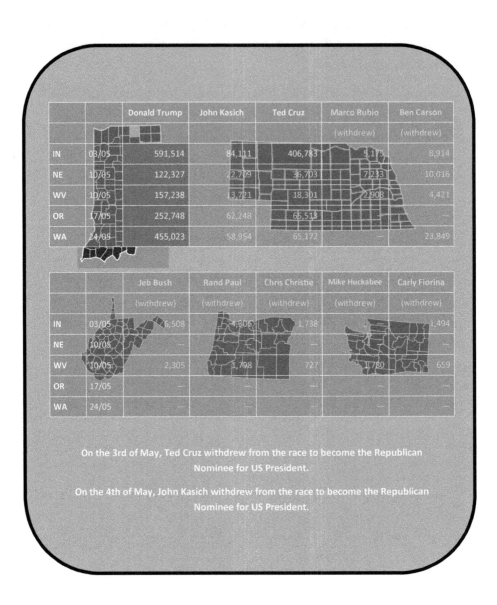

		Donald Trump	John Kasich	Ted Cruz	Marco Rubio (withdrew)	Ben Carson (withdrew)
IN	03/05	591,514	84,111	406,783	5,175	8,914
NE	10/05	122,327	22,709	36,703	7,233	10,016
WV	10/05	157,238	13,721	18,301	2,908	4,421
OR	17/05	252,748	62,248	65,513	—	—
WA	24/05	455,023	58,954	65,172	—	23,849

		Jeb Bush (withdrew)	Rand Paul (withdrew)	Chris Christie (withdrew)	Mike Huckabee (withdrew)	Carly Fiorina (withdrew)
IN	03/05	6,508	4,306	1,738	—	1,494
NE	10/05	—	—	—	—	—
WV	10/05	2,305	1,798	727	1,780	659
OR	17/05	—	—	—	—	—
WA	24/05	—	—	—	—	—

On the 3rd of May, Ted Cruz withdrew from the race to become the Republican Nominee for US President.

On the 4th of May, John Kasich withdrew from the race to become the Republican Nominee for US President.

MAY 2016

VENUES OF TRUMP'S SPEECHES

01/05	Rally	Terre Haute, IN
01/05	Rally	Fort Wayne, IN
02/05	Rally	Carmel, IN
02/05	Rally	South Bend, IN
05/05	Rally	Charleston, WV
06/05	Rally	Omaha, NE
06/05	Rally	Eugene, OR
07/06	Rally	Spokane, WA
07/05	Rally	Lynden, WA

19/05	Rally	Lawrenceville, NJ
24/05	Rally	Albuquerque, NM
25/05	Rally	Anaheim, CA
26/05	Speech	Bismarck, ND
26/05	Rally	Billings, MT
27/05	Rally	Fresno, CA
27/05	Rally	San Diego, CA
31/05	Speech	Trump Tower, NY

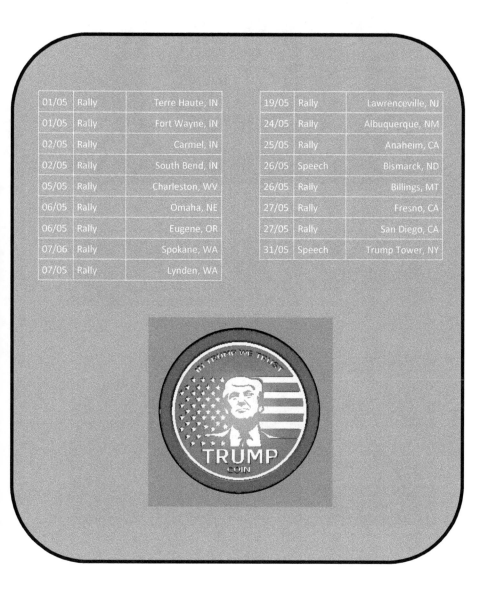

TrumpCoin—Make Crypto Great Again

FOUNDER OF TRUMPCOIN RESIGNED FROM THE LEAD PROJECT MANAGER ROLE

JUNE 2016

I. Promotional video "What is TrumpCoin?" uploaded to YouTube.

II. A new lead project manager took over from user "chicken65".

III. Plan outlined by user "CantStump" to move TrumpCoin forward.

IV. Ownership of the domain http://trumpcoin.com secured.

V. Surge in the market capitalisation occurred during the last week.

On the first day of June, a discussion took place about whether a brand new Bitcointalk thread would be necessary once the coin shifted towards Trump Ethereum in the future. This was viewed as low priority at the time.

Also on the first day at 20:14:46 UTC, user "bitbullbarbados" said he had been busy collating all relevant and important websites associated with the coin. Some of these were the following:

> http://trumpcoin.rocks
> http://www.makemoneygreatagain.org/
> https://twitter.com/TRUMPCOIN1
> https://www.reddit.com/r/trumpcoin
> https://www.facebook.com/TRUMPcoincryptocurrency/

JUNE 2016

Other websites he thought of as important were:

> http://www.makecryptogreatagain.org/Content/Community/
> http://coinmarketcap.com/currencies/trumpcoin/
> http://buytrumpcoin.com/
> http://princajaba.wix.com/trumpdeals
> https://poloniex.com/coinRequest
> https://www.donaldjtrump.com/
> http://www.diamondandsilkinc.com/
> https://www.trumpdollar.us/
> https://www.youtube.com/watch?v=iMM-X0mDonI&feature=youtu.be
> https://www.youtube.com/channel/UCrvedbf2mAUNj5aKveULVbA
> https://c-cex.com/?p=trump-btc
> https://yobit.net/en/trade/TRUMP/BTC
> https://safecex.com/market?q=TRUMP/BTC

On the 7th of June, another TrumpCoin promotional video had been created by user "TrumpCoinContent". It was titled "What is TrumpCoin?". Before uploading it, he wanted user "chicken65" to check it and recommend any tweaks. It describes the purpose of the coin, what cryptocurrency is and how the Trump Fund works. A second video planned would detail how to buy TrumpCoin and the third would present the philosophy behind the coin. On the same day at 18:36:36 UTC, user "TrumpCoinContent" announced the following:

> "OFFICIAL TRUMPCOIN PROMO VIDEO
> https://www.youtube.com/watch?v=0A0KzoFuOLQ
>
> Here ya go ladies and gents
>
> If you feel like kindly donating to the content creator, here's the address:
> TLPSDWJfbZmHUf4oGEA4YKpKNN49toypyE
> (this address ONLY takes TRUMP please do not send bitcoin through this address)
>
> Cheers boys and girls, MAGA"

JUNE 2016

What follows is the full transcript of the video "What is TrumpCoin?". As soon as it was uploaded, user "TrumpCoinContent" was publicly congratulated for his work. In early October, it had been viewed by approximately 20,250 people.

Narrator: "Let me ask you something… What if there was a way you could financially support the Trump campaign without giving away all your money, and make a profit at the same time? That'd sound like a pretty tremendous deal, right? Yeah that's what we thought too. Meet TrumpCoin, the world's first cryptocurrency designed in honour of future president Donald J Trump"

News Reporter: "As the Dollar and the Euro continue their slow path to recovery, some people are trading in their money for currency that is already booming. It's called Bitcoin."

Narrator: "Most of us have heard of Bitcoin. It's a cryptocurrency, a currency that only exists in computers and gets traded back and forth between people all over the world. What you might not know is, there are hundreds of other cryptocurrencies out there, Ethereum, Dogecoin, Litecoin… you get the idea. But what does this have to do with Trump? Well earlier I promised you would be able to support the Trump campaign with TrumpCoins, now here's how that works. Currently there are 6 million TrumpCoins in existence. 200,000 of these have been set aside in the Trump Fund. The Trump Fund will be donated to the Trump campaign once it reaches a substantial value. See, cryptocurrencies get traded on exchanges, similar to how the stock market works. The only difference is cryptos are traded in Bitcoins instead of dollars. People buy and sell cryptos using Bitcoin, and supply and demand ultimately dictates the price of each coin. So, if a lot of people get interested in the TrumpCoin Project and buy the coins, the value of all the coins goes up, and the value of the Trump Fund goes up as well. But the best part is, unlike a donation where you never see your money again, when you buy TrumpCoins, you now own those TrumpCoins. If the value of TrumpCoin doubles, you could sell them back onto the market and make a 100% profit. You win, Trump wins, America wins."

Donald Trump: "We will have so much winning if I get elected that you may get bored with winning."

Narrator: "Remember, the TrumpCoin Project will only be a success if everyone does their part and we get the word out to all Trump fans out there. If you need more help or you run into any problems, you can speak to the TrumpCoin Team any time either on the website or in the discussion thread. The links are below in the description. Good luck and let's Make America Great Again!"

JUNE 2016

On the 15th of June at 21:13:04 UTC, user "chicken65" said:

> "In a couple of weeks I will have no more time to handle the daily goings on of this project. So, it is with sadness that I have to announce that I will be resigning as the project dev 2 weeks from today. I will look for someone to take over the project but anyone who is interested please state on the forum (no pm's please, I wont answer). Whoever takes over will have to be 100% trustworthy because you will be in control of the Trump Fund. ID Verification will be nescessary but of course will never be revealed by me unless you run with the campiagn donation fund.
>
> Aside from my own business sufferring quite a bit in doing this project, I was committed many months ago to begin work on a large project and their banging on the door. Contracts were signed so I have to keep up my end of the bargain. I cannot do this project and that one at the same time.
>
> As of now Im just an investor like everyone else. However, I will keep trying to secure Trumps endorsement/acknowledgement. That side wont change. Im just talking about the forum stuff, website, twitter, emails etc.
>
> I have very much enjoyed the project and its really great to see a community working together on this project. Keep at it and the gold will come..
> ill still be around for 2 weeks and will pop in now and then to support the project. It is of course in my interest to do that.
>
> Respect to you all!"

People respected user "chicken65" for his decision. In particular, user "signal7" had seen many Project Lead Developers who had just got bored and disappeared without a trace. He had never seen someone give a two week resignation from that position. On the 15th of June at 22:50:21 UTC, user "Signal7" was quoted as saying:

> "Thank you for this Chicken and for all of the work that you have put into this project. I wish you the very best.
>
> This isn't the end. It's a new beginning. I'm still in."

JUNE 2016

On the 16th of June, some members of the community did not care who became the new lead project manager, as long as the project kept going. With immediate effect, on the same day at 05:41:06 UTC, user "chicken65" said:

> "I can think of no one better for the position than you. Ladies and gentlemen, patriots and crypto enthusiasts meet your new project manager: CantStump
>
> I can definitely say he will bring a fresh new approach to the project and believe me he's a dedicated guy. He was almost solely responsible for promoting Trump on Yobits troll box during the first few weeks of heavy dumping by a few Tump hating miners potentially saving the coin from disaster with his relentless enthusiasm and promotion of the Trump Coin. He hasn't dumped coins (i know for a fact). He will be a tremendous asset to all of us and the project. All hail CANTSTUMP!
>
> Im going full political in the background. I will not rest until we secure Trumps endorsement. Its simply a role switch. Im very happy I can concentrate on that side. It was always my area which I havent been able to fully exploit.
>
> PS Change of command will happen with a fortnight, maybe sooner."

On the following day at 00:46:32 UTC, user "CantStump" described his appointment as a tremendous honour and appreciated the hard work user "chicken65" had put in so far. He promised a formal announcement of his acceptance of the role and would soon release a plan outlining future tasks (marketing and tech). He said:

> I've been with this project since close to the beginning and have been a Trump supporter since July last year. Ever since Mr Trump took his now famous escalator ride at Trump Tower I knew there may never be a man more awe-inspiring than The Donald himself, and he has never let me down to this day.

He was keen to delegate tasks to a dedicated community who wanted success.

There were some reservations and curiosity why user "CantStump" had been chosen because he had not posted regularly on the official TrumpCoin Bitcointalk thread. Perhaps he had had great communications via other mediums with user "chicken65" and others. On the 18th of June, user "CantStump" submitted another post on the original Trumpcoin Bitcointalk thread in which he outlined "things to deal with" in the immediate future. Appealing to the community as a whole, he knew the potential of the coin and that a common goal was shared:

> "To ensure a substantial donation to the Trump Campaign and to help Mr Trump Make America Great Again. If we want to secure Trumpcoin's place in history and have the Trump Fund make a real difference then we will need a plan."

Going forward, the plan was to build up the Trumpcoin Team by delegating well-defined roles. This would allow responsibility for different aspects of the project to be delegated to the right people for the job while maintaining a common direction for everyone involved. Anyone interested in joining the team was encouraged to come forward, introduce him/herself and say how s/he would contribute to the project. Popular people such as users "Signal7" and "indiemax" even more so.

On the 19th of June at 20:52:33 UTC, user "chicken65" submitted his last post as the lead project manager in which he thanked everyone for their continued support. He said user "CantStump" would take his role within the next 24 hours. User "chicken65" was still the holder of the 200k Trump Fund (viewed by him as the safest way) and was looking forward to a future endorsement of TrumpCoin from the official Donald Trump Campaign Team.

On the 21st of June, user "CantStump" outlined the plan for the following week. In no particular order, these were:

1. To amend portions of the content on the official website.
2. To implement a proper organisational structure of the TrumpCoin Team.
3. To receive as many potential/innovative marketing ideas as possible.

On the 25th of June, user "chicken65" said the "two week hand over is done" and he was no longer going to post on the original Trumpcoin Bitcointalk thread as the "lead dev". He emphasised ten points which the new team could possibly work on:

> 1. New moderated thread
> 2. New official Twitter account handled by CantStump (important) which everyone needs to support (crucial).
> 3. Memes memes and then some - all aimed directly to Trumps closest, his campaign team,
> 4. Start the Superpac
> 5. Increase the Trump Fund (Crucial)
> 6. Enough with the multipe websites. Totally not needed.
> 7. Personal message to the largest Trump Coin holder.
> 8. Slush Fund - How many times do I need to reepat this.
> 9. I cant say because newbies and infiltrators will start hitting that person up - Game Over
> 10. Create a Superpac - Best idea ive seen in about 100 pages of the thread.

He emphasised the importance of the coin as a Trump Supporters Campaign Donation Project/Superpac more than just an ordinary cryptocurrency. He said he would stay in communication with the new lead project manager in case of any substantial problems arose. He was relieved to remove himself from the hateful fud messages and weirdos on Skype.

Two days later at 08:31:34 UTC, user "CantStump" had some major updates to announce. One of these concerned the official website:

> "The unbelievably dedicated Trump fan bitbullbarbados has secured ownership of the domain http://trumpcoin.com to be used for this project. He achieved this through his own negotiation with the previous owner and with the use of his own fiat, which was a serious amount of money.
>
> This is incredible news and we all owe bitbullbarbados a major debt of gratitude for a first class job!! A big thanks also to Signal7 for his extensive efforts on the tech side (which I'll go into more detail about later in the week)."

JUNE 2016

The new domain was quickly made to re-direct to http://trumpcoin.rocks while it was being designed. User "bitbullbarbados" was politely asked to post his wallet address so that others could, if they wished, donate cryptocurrency to him.

The other update concerned the organisational structure of the TrumpCoin Team. Several positions had already been filled. User "CantStump" was happy to clarify the fact that everyone on this team had contributed greatly to the coin:

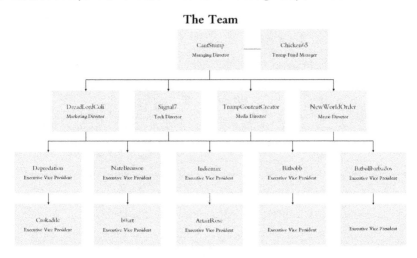

Something else to look forward to was a "How To Buy" video from user "TrumpCoinContent" who said it would be ready in about ten days time.

During the last week of June, the market capitalisation was surging:

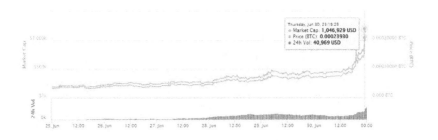

JUNE 2016

Historical values for the last four days of June from YoBit and C-Cex were as follows:

	Price	Low	Open	Close	High	Volume (TRUMP)
27th June (YB)	5,047	4,300	4,837	5,257	5,700	148,787.08
27th June (CC)	5,529	4,750	5,259	5,799	6,101	92,444.78
28th June (YB)	6,343.5	5,000	5,354	7,333	7,967	278,823.96
28th June (CC)	6,812	5,201	5,799	7,825	8,787	136,446.40
29th June (YB)	7,911	6,313	7,499	8,323	9,000	213,495.46
29th June (CC)	8,120	7,747	7,827	8,413	13,120	133,820.02
30th June (YB)	15,965	8,390	8,890	23,040	25,020	326,374.13
30th June (CC)	16,606.5	7,777	8,413	24,800	24,800	138,821.25

source: www.cryptocompare.com

As a consequence of the surge in the Bitcoin Satoshi value of one unit of TRUMP account, the market capitalisation of TrumpCoin surpassed $1 million for the first time on the 30th of June (1 TRUMP = ~$0.165).

Over the past couple of weeks, user "CantStump" was impressed by the immense amount of energy, smart organisational skills and professionalism inherent in the community. In his opinion, if sustained, there would be no limit to success.

Other events which occurred in the month of June were:

- On the 3rd of June, user "NewWorldOrder" thanked the community for their support in helping to get three Facebook Advertisements paid for.

- On the 9th of June, user "TrumpCoinContent" created another Facebook page which is currently the official page for the coin.

- On the 25th of June, user "chicken65" was slightly disheartened to see that very little had been done to get the attention of the Trump Campaign Team.

JUNE 2016

GOP PRIMARY/CAUCUS RESULTS

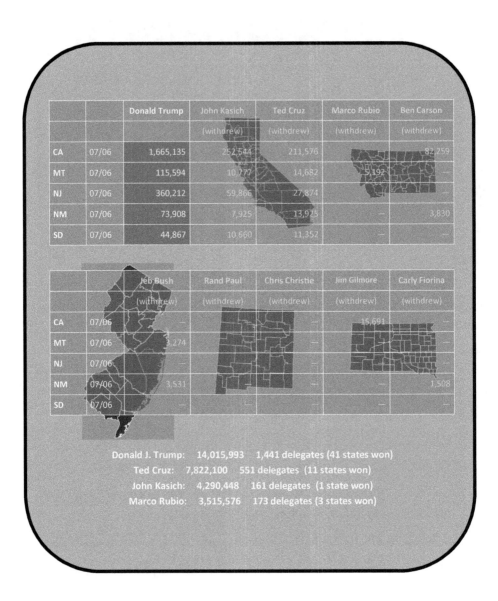

		Donald Trump	John Kasich (withdrew)	Ted Cruz (withdrew)	Marco Rubio (withdrew)	Ben Carson (withdrew)
CA	07/06	1,665,135	252,544	211,576	—	82,259
MT	07/06	115,594	10,777	14,682	5,192	—
NJ	07/06	360,212	59,866	27,874	—	—
NM	07/06	73,908	7,925	13,925	—	3,830
SD	07/06	44,867	10,660	11,352	—	—

		Jeb Bush (withdrew)	Rand Paul (withdrew)	Chris Christie (withdrew)	Jim Gilmore (withdrew)	Carly Fiorina (withdrew)
CA	07/06	—	—	—	15,691	—
MT	07/06	1,274	—	—	—	—
NJ	07/06	—	—	—	—	—
NM	07/06	3,531	—	—	—	1,508
SD	07/06	—	—	—	—	—

Donald J. Trump: 14,015,993 1,441 delegates (41 states won)
Ted Cruz: 7,822,100 551 delegates (11 states won)
John Kasich: 4,290,448 161 delegates (1 state won)
Marco Rubio: 3,515,576 173 delegates (3 states won)

JUNE 2016

VENUES OF TRUMP'S SPEECHES

01/06	Rally	Sacramento, CA
02/06	Rally	San Jose, CA
03/06	Rally	Redding, CA
10/06	Rally	Richmond, VA
11/06	Rally	Tampa, FL
11/06	Rally	Moon Township, PA
13/06	Speech	Manchester, NH
14/06	Rally	Greensboro, NC
15/06	Rally	Atlanta, GA
16/06	Rally	Dallas, TX
17/06	Rally	Houston, TX
17/06	Rally	The Woodlands, TX
18/06	Rally	Las Vegas, NV
18/06	Rally	Phoenix, AZ
22/06	Speech	New York, NY
28/06	Speech	Monessen, PA
28/06	Rally	St. Clairsville, OH
29/06	Rally	Bangor, ME
30/06	Speech	Manchester, NH

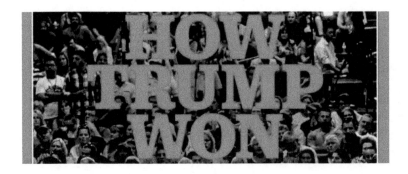

JULY 2016

A NEW TRUMPCOIN LLC TEAM ESTABLISHED
JULY 2016

I. All time high market capitalisation of TrumpCoin was attained.
II. TrumpCoin became TrumpCoin LLC.
III. User "DreadLordColi" was voted in as the temporary treasurer.
IV. New dedicated block explorer at http://chain.blockpioneers.info/trump.
V. A recently assembled TrumpCoin Team unveiled.

Following on from the last week of June, the market capitalisation of the coin continued to increase until it reached an all time high on the 1st of July 2016. According to the website www.coinmarketcap.com, a value of ~$1,243,470 was attained with a corresponding (average over the exchanges) Bitcoin Satoshi value of 27,961 per unit TRUMP. As can be seen below, the rise in value was substantial:

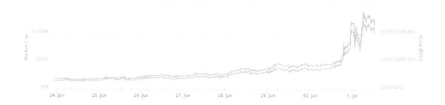

At the time of publication of this book, this high was never reached again.

JULY 2016

On the 1st of July at 06:30:40 UTC, user "Depredation" noticed that TrumpCoin had reached top position in terms of 24 hour % increase in market capitalisation:

"Highest 24 hour change on market cap. Well done."

#	Name	Market Cap	Price	Available Supply	Volume (24h)	% Change (24h)	Price Graph (7d)
53	TrumpCoin	$ 1,243,093	$ 0.191188	6,501,342 TRUMP	$ 69,686	242.82 %	
12	Emercoin	$ 17,425,834	$ 0.458331	38,020,195 EMC	$ 296,542	168.26 %	
78	Nexus	$ 642,813	$ 0.016427	39,131,959 NXS	$ 17,631	56.99 %	
70	AmberCoin	$ 724,704	$ 0.016678	43,452,451 AMBER **	$ 196	56.65 %	
76	HempCoin	$ 648,976	$ 0.000479	1,354,638,638 HMP	$ 10,260	49.71 %	
55	Yocoin	$ 1,101,396	$ 0.056909	19,353,800 YOC	$ 61,174	42.38 %	
56	Expanse	$ 1,056,934	$ 0.511550	2,066,139 EXP	$ 615,448	39.33 %	

On the following day, a growing number of people began to worry about the absence of user "CantStump". There were also problems with the official block explorer (owned/maintained by user "TrumpTechGuy") and issues with the blockchain not syncing (downloading onto people's computers) fully. It became apparent that the server on which the block explorer resided had gone off line.

There were calls for user "Signal7" to become the new lead project manager as confidence in the recently formed team continued to wane. As a result of the malfunctional official block explorer, members of community wondered if a hard fork would be necessary in order to move things forward.

Also on the 2nd of July, user "chicken65" made the new Trump Fund wallet address public for the community:

TDAJpGdnatgeeY1GuEhDhbmgXaSf3WU7Ai (New Trump Fund Address)

JULY 2016

By making the wallet address of the Trump Fund public, user "chicken65" was trying to dispel the accusations he was selling it. User "Signal7", who was the "Technical Director" of the coin at the time, was finding communication with user "chicken65" very difficult (3 days without contact now). Also, he was finding communication with user "TrumpTechGuy" very unreliable. He was keen to sort out the lacklustre state of affairs.

On the 2nd of July at 17:39:09 UTC, user "Signal7" said:

> "We can still fix it. If the original devs refuse to help, we can, as a community agree to officially fork and take back control. That is the beauty of open source and decentralization. I have a personal copy of every version of both the V1 and V2 sources. I recommend that anyone that knows how to fork a copy of the GIT do so now, in case it does get taken down by the owner(s).
>
> It's not too late and we can recover from this situation one way or another. I hope that it happens in a peaceful and professional way."

On the other hand, user "chicken65" gave his opinion on the current circumstances. On the same day at 22:37:53 UTC, he was quoted as saying:

> "Im going to wait to hear from CantStump. I may have to start firing people and take charge again - despite the fact I totally do not have the time. But I will not allow Daddy be tarnished!
>
> Chain is totally fine. The explorer is again being rebuilt as we speak. If it doesnt work properly this time we will use an off the shelf one. The one currently in use was coded specifically for the coin so yeah, it may have some bugs."

User "chicken65" made it clear he was not making any decisions on behalf of the new team, but only held the Trump Fund until other arrangements could be made. He was still trying to gain official endorsement of TrumpCoin.

JULY 2016

On the 3rd of July, the original TrumpCoin Bitcointalk thread was beginning to attract a growing number of "newbies". Some of these people were genuine supporters, whereas others were obvious fudsters/trolls etc. It had got to the point at which user "chicken65" decided to create a new moderated thread:

> 2nd official TRUMP Bitcointalk thread created: 3rd of July 2016 at 04:16:01 UTC
>
> 1st official TRUMP Bitcointalk thread locked: 3rd of July 2016 at 04:30:30 UTC
>
> 1st official TRUMP Bitcointalk thread re-opened: 3rd of July 2016 UTC at 20:27:50 UTC

One reason why the original thread had been re-opened was to allow the community there to work towards transferring the Trump Fund to an elected, high profile and trusted third party entity. This would be the case until a proper treasury was established. Both users "chicken65" and "Signal7" agreed to proceed calmly towards a mutual resolution.

At the time, user "Signal7" wanted to hold the Trump Fund in a clean new address at TGyL5KXE4FdEUG1UAQ677aSamwCYcihGcn, whereas user "chicken65" preferred to send the coins to a proper and professional escrow service.

On the 3rd of July at 21:12:31 UTC, user "Signal7" responded to user "chicken65":

> "While I feel it is the coin's best interest for you to absolve yourself of responsibility, I also know that you are the founder and I respect you as such. I strongly believe this project can go down in history with you recognized as the one who started it. I do not wish to see you leave. I only wish to secure trust with our investors. I know you to be an honest and passionate individual who has done many great things here. We are on the doorstep of big league. If we can establish trust for all, we will assuredly walk through that door."

It was now known that user "CantStump" had stepped down. User "chicken65" was sorry he selected him as the lead project manager without properly vetting him and accused him of intentionally hyping the price in June.

JULY 2016

A decision was made by user "chicken65" to transfer the entire 200k Trump Fund into Escrow. Firstly, user "chicken65" sent 100,000 TRUMP directly to user "Signal7". Once both 100,000 TRUMP sums had been transferred into escrow, user "chicken65" was not bothered if user "Signal7" took control of the coin and he would no longer concern himself with the coin.

On the 4th of July at 18:14:57 UTC, user "SebastianJu" was quoted as saying:

> "Hi everyone, I do not know what the past conversation is about but I was asked to come in here and confirm that chicken65 asked me to hold 100k TrumpCoin in escrow on c-cex.com. I gave him my deposit address and he sent 50k TrumpCoin there and told me he will send the other half later.
>
> Just as a headsup. If there is something that I need to know as an escrow then let me know by pm since I do not have the time to follow the various threads on the forum."

User "chicken65" was now waiting for user "Signal7" to send his recently received 100,000 TRUMP to the escrow address NQEBXWJBQ3U15kXxUik1dDvWkttcBoDXa (a C-Cex wallet address created by user "SebastianJu"). Unfortunately, user "Signal7" refused to do that. Subsequently, a dispute between them began. It was at this time that user "chicken65" revealed his true identity. He requested user "Signal7" to do the same.

On the 4th of July at 23:45:43 UTC, user "chicken65" locked the original TrumpCoin Bitcointalk thread once and for all. He posted a statement which initially read:

> "At this time I have no choice but to lock this thread for good. Despite it being only a handful of trouble makers they are still making enough noise to make the situation intolerable to deal with. As time goes on the fud will just become more and more. Its a lot of fud to deal with. We have PND group fud, we have Trump haters signing up simply because they see this as a way to vent their hatred and we have general newbie fud who buy in to much of the lies thats been spread about this project and me. This had to stop."

User "chicken65" was happy to leave the project if the community wanted him to.

JULY 2016

On the 5th of July at 03:21:43 UTC, user "chicken65" said:

> "Revealing my ID is already beginning to bring in dividends (more on that in a later post). it was always bothersome to me that I was anonymous but i just carried on like that through Crypto Scene habit I guess. Anyway, it frees me up to do interviews and actually speak to people. No waywould we get acknowledgement from Trump without this. I sort of always knew that, but I guess better late than never."

Some members of the community apologised to user "chicken65" for their remarks which they said were based on untruths and rushed accusations.

On the 5th of July at 13:35:15 UTC, user "Signal7" said:

> "I would like to come to a consensus of fair terms to move this project forward with full transparency and legitimacy.
>
> My goal is not to simply oust Chicken. I wish for a level playing field and truth in advertising. That is all I am after."

User "TrumpCoinContent" was still interested in remaining on board as the media content producer for the coin. Also, user "TrumpInfo" wanted to know if he could apply for a position on the team.

On the 7th of July, the block explorer at http://www.vicenet.org:3001/ continued to be the only known and trusted one available.

There had been a great number of announcements during the first week of July.

After a few days, user "Signal7" posted the following:

> "Looking a little tense around here this morning.
>
> Guys, stay with me through today/tomorrow. I have been taking legal steps to protect us all. These things take time. I do have some very wonderful news and updates coming but I cannot release anything until I complete one last very important task today.
>
> We will begin voting this week, among lots more.
>
> Hang in there. Significant updates coming today, tomorrow at the very latest."

Users "bitinator", "Jaerky", "BitBobb" and "Depredation" were excited and enthusiastic to see Trumpcoin striving to become more authentic and transparent.

On the 11th of July at 15:36:09 UTC, user "Signal7" said:

> "TrumpCoin is now officially TrumpCoin, LLC
>
> SCC ID: S6276572
>
> License: https://sccefile.scc.virginia.gov/Documents/1607115301.pdf?documentName=Attestation
>
> More news to come…"

According to Wikipedia, the definition of a LLC (Limited Liability Company) is:

> "It is the United States-specific form of a private limited company. It is a business structure that combines the pass-through taxation of a partnership or sole proprietorship with the limited liability of a corporation.[1] An LLC is not a corporation; it is a legal form of a company that provides limited liability to its owners in many jurisdictions."

Yet again, praise was given to user "Signal7" for his continued dedication to the TrumpCoin Project.

JULY 2016

On the 12th of July, user "Signal7" notified the community that the official website at http://trumpcoin.com had been updated. He asked supporters of the coin to read and report any grammatical errors or inaccuracies. Another major update was promised to occur at a tentative time in the future (everyone can participate in).

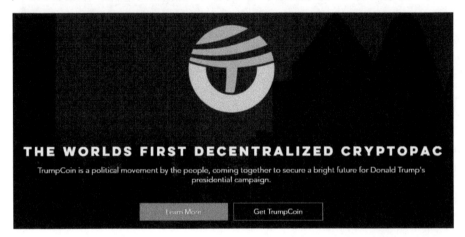

On the following day, user "Signal7" told the community he had wanted to file a "Statement of Organization" to move forward with a certifiably legitimate Super PAC to support Donald Trump for president. However, at least one official treasurer (an employee and/or agent of TrumpCoin LLC) was required beforehand. This person had to be a US National. A discussion followed about the legality of forming a real superPAC.

On the 14th of July at 14:56:14 UTC, a result was known from an online 24h poll:

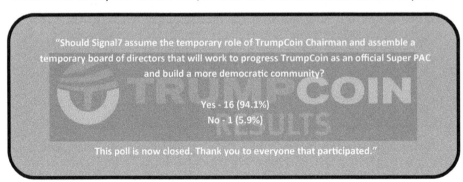

As soon as user "Signal7" had assumed the position of temporary chairman, he began to message potential nominees for positions on the temporary board of directors. An important position to fill, as mentioned earlier, was temporary treasurer. The first two users to become nominees were "Bitbobb" and "Depredation". User "Signal7" was awaiting a response from user "DreadLordColi" as to whether or not he was interested.

Over the next couple of days, there were provocateurs and saboteurs who were keen to give user "Bitbobb" a bad reputation. This consumed over ten pages (over two hundred posts) on the second official TrumpCoin Bitcointalk thread.

On the 18th of July at 18:01:23 UTC, user "Signal7" announced the following:

> "The poll is now open for Temporary Treasurer of TrumpCoin. Once chosen, the Temporary Treasurer will play a vital role in the efforts to firmly establish the TrumpCoin Project as a legitimate and transparent organization that supports Donald Trump for President and the advancement of blockchain technologies as a means for bypassing special interests in government, namely in our elections.
>
> This poll should not be misunderstood to be a binding election. It is an opinion poll to allow the TrumpCoin community to help guide me towards choosing a trusted and respected community member for this important role. I respectfully reserve the right to reject the outcome of this poll pending vetting and background checks to follow."

After approximately 24 hours, the Bitcointalk poll closed. On the 19th of July at 17:18:29 UTC, user "Signal7" congratulated user "DreadLordColi" after which he said it would take a day or two setup his accounts, pending vetting and checks. Full results of the online Bitcointalk poll were as follows:

Poll
Question: Who should be the Temporary Treasurer of TrumpCoin?

DreadLordColi	9 (50%)
Depredation	3 (16.7%)
BitBobb	4 (22.2%)
Bitinator	2 (11.1%)
Other (Comment Below)	0 (0%)
Total Voters: 18	

JULY 2016

On the 20th of July at 14:01:03 UTC, user "Signal7" said:

> "The next step is to consolidate threads into a fresh new central ANN (today). After that is Roll Call for the new team. The team will spend a few days going over my proposals, making corrections as necessary with a goal of publishing the new roadmap.
> Then we follow the roadmap."

Without the use of an online poll, an almost unanimous decision was taken to go ahead with a new moderated official TrumpCoin Bitcointalk thread. On the 20th of July at 16:11:26 UTC, user "Signal7" said:

> "New moderated ANN thread created to consolidate and organize all other TrumpCoin related threads. https://bitcointalk.org/index.php?topic=1558916.msg15649610
> This should serve as the new main thread."

To be exact, this new thread titled "[ANN] [TRUMP] [MODERATED] TrumpCoin SuperPAC" had been created on the 20th of July at 16:00:25 UTC. User "Signal7" felt it was important to moderate it so as to help sustain a productive atmosphere of conversation. Only posts deemed to be seriously offensive, degrading and "troll like" would be deleted without anyone's freedom of speech being impeded.

As a response to ongoing accusations that the coin was a scam, user "Signal7" highlighted legitimate tasks which counteracted these claims:

> 1. I have already publicly registered an LLC to my own identity, which is now publicly available on my SCC filing.
> 2. We are preparing filings now for the FEC which will make my ID even more public along with Dread's.
> 3. We really are starting a SuperPAC to campaign for Donald Trump legally and transparently.
> 4. We plan to leverage our PAC to push for better FEC acceptance of crypto. What part of any of this is a scam?

JULY 2016

On the 22nd of July at 07:52:05 UTC, user "Bitbobb" publicly announced the first t-shirt available to purchase 100% payable in TrumpCoin. On the following day, he advertised a second t-shirt also payable 100% in TRUMP. These were:

1st; "Abraham Drinking"   2nd; "Made In U.S.A."

On the 24th of July at 05:44:15 UTC, user "DreadLordColi" was proud to unveil the recently assembled team of talented and eager individuals. Both himself and user "Signal7" thought this was necessary in order to help move TrumpCoin forward. Two members of the TrumpCoin Development Team were:

Jason Bobbitt (user "Signal7") — Lead Developer & Chief Technical Officer
Colin H. (user "DreadLordColi") — Treasurer & Director of Digital Marketing

Six other individuals, referred to collectively as "TrumpCoin Staff", were:

Robert W. (user "Depredation") — Community Outreach
John M. (user "TrumpCoinContent") — Media Content Manager
Gregory P. (user "TrumpInfo") — Economic Advisor
Alex B. (user "Doogjy") — Social Media Co-ordinator
Scott H. (user "Bitbobb") — Ad Hoc Merchandiser
Alex G. (user "Hiatus") — Designer

The current TrumpCoin Team can be seen on pages 24 and 25.

JULY 2016

On the 26th of July, there were calls for user "chicken65" to implement a "301 redirect" so that the old official website domain at http://trumpcoin.rocks would redirect to the new official website at http://trumpcoin.com. The current team were happy to help user "chicken65" if he was unsure how to proceed. Two days later, user "chicken65" said he was not in control of the server on which the site resided. He had tried to contact the person who was, but to no avail.

On the last day of the month, user "bitbullbarbados" stressed the importance of promoting TrumpCoin as much as possible to as many people as possible. As had been evident before, there were those people who had been working hard to bring the coin down. There were now 100 days until the election with Donald Trump and Mike Pence confirmed as the official presidential and vice-presidential nominees.

Other events which occurred in the month of July were:

- On the 19th of July, a new dedicated block explorer for TrumpCoin was created by user "BanzaiBTC" at http://chain.blockpioneers.info/trump/. It was described as beautiful by user "Depredation" and professional by user "Bitbobb".

- To coincide with Donald J. Trump humbly and gratefully accepting the Republican Nomination for President on the 21st of July, a new official TrumpCoin Twitter account at http://twitter.com/TrumpCoinTweets/ was created.

- On the 21st of July, user "SebastianJu" sent the 100k (halve of the Trump Fund) back to user "chicken65".

- On the 26th of July, a new ".info" website was made available to help newcomers. Also on this day, http://trumpcoin.com was newly redesigned.

JULY 2016

VENUES OF TRUMP'S SPEECHES

01/07	Speech	Denver, CO
05/07	Rally	Raleigh, NC
06/07	Rally	Cincinnati, OH
11/07	Speech	Veterans Reform
12/07	Rally	Westfield, IN
16/07	Rally	Zionsville, IN
20/07	Speech	Cleveland, OH
21/07	Speech	GOP NC, OH
25/07	Town Hall	Roonoke, VA
25/07	Rally	Winston-Salem, NC
26/07	Speech	Charlotte, NC
27/07	Town Hall	Scranton, PA
27/07	Rally	Toledo, OH
28/07	Raly	Davenport, IA
28/07	Rally	Cedar Rapids, IA
29/07	Rally	Colorado Springs, CO
29/07	Rally	Denver, CO

On the 15th of July, Mike Pence was officially selected as the vice presidential running mate to Donald J. Trump.

On the 18th-21st of July, the 2016 Republican National Convention was held at the Quicken Loans Arena in Cleveland, Ohio (OH). There were 2,472 delegates there who formerly nominated Donald J. Trump as the Republicans choice for President of the United States.

Of the 19 speakers billed as "headliners" at the GOP National Convention, six were members of the Trump family: Trump himself, his wife Melania and four of his children, Ivanka, Don Jr., Eric and Tiffany.

TrumpCoin—Make Crypto Great Again

FURTHER PROMOTION OF TRUMPCOIN
AUGUST 2016

I. A statement from the founder of TrumpCoin publicly issued.

II. Video titled "MAGA: Join The Fight For America" uploaded to YouTube.

III. Altcoin Today article about TrumpCoin published online.

IV. Another block explorer created at https://www.blockexperts.com/trump.

V. No posts from user "Signal7" during the last three weeks of August.

As a means to promote further transparency throughout the community, user "Signal7" announced his intentions to make the Trump Fund more secure. On the 1st of August at 12:58:49 UTC, he was quoted as saying:

> "You will see the Trump Funds moving around today as I move the coins into the new permanent Trump Fund wallet address, which is TSt65isKg47WXPEXa7Rq866QCTNxYFL2CB. The new wallet exists in a highly secure PCI DSS Level 1 server environment and supports our needs for shared access with checks and balances like purchase orders, expense and sales reporting, invoicing, receipts, and approval/release chains.
>
> Once the move is complete, the fund can be monitored by everyone here: http://chain.blockpioneers.info/trump/search.php?id=TSt65isKg47WXPEXa7Rq866QCTNxYFL2CB
>
> I will be providing updates later tonight with more details."

Some members of the community respected user "Signal7" for his initial warning of the transfer. They described it as professional behaviour. It was also a nice way to "fend off the fudsters" who would have probably accused the TrumpCoin Team of selling the Trump Fund. Again, the 100,000 TRUMP held by user "chicken65" was still not included.

On the 2nd of August at 01:00:58 UTC, user "Depredation" said:

> "Great news, I can't wait to use the tipbot"

This was a response to the news that TrumpCoin would have its very own Reddit TipBot in the next few days. At this time, it was undergoing extensive tests to ensure optimal future functionality.

Also on the 2nd of August, a discussion took place about whether to publicly acknowledge user "chicken65" as the original founder of the coin. A suggestion was to include him on the official TrumpCoin Team list on the official website. On that same day at 21:41:35 UTC, user "chicken65" was quoted as saying:

> **Statement From The Founder of Trump Coin**
>
> "As some of you know I was the one who launched Trump Coin and as far as Im concerned this is a very different project now. Or to put it more accurately, this is a group of people doing their own thing using Trumps name and a project I launched to promote a coin they are heavily invested in. Still, I have no problem with that at all."

User "chicken65" also referred back to when he sent 100,000 TRUMP of the Trump Fund to user "Signal7". According to user "chicken65", user "Signal7" did not honour the agreement to send his 100,000 TRUMP into escrow, whereas user "chicken65" did. After much deliberation, user "chicken65" decided to hold on to his half of the fund and eventually donate it to the cause originally intended. He was the founder, so he thought he was well within his rights to do that.

On the 4th of August at 01:30:50 UTC, user "Signal7" said:

"We are rolling out a few really cool updates over the next few days.
We begin with TrumpCoinContents's latest masterpiece promotional video.

https://www.youtube.com/watch?v=WvBDCBOjDwk

Enjoy the new vid and stay tuned.

TCC, we all know how hard you have worked on this. I don't know how you can stay up for 40 hours at a time. Your dedication and passion are unmatched.
Please post your TrumpCoin address for donations.

See you all tomorrow." 😊

Once again, members of the community congratulated user "TrumpCoinContent" for a brilliant, amazing and high energy video. In particular, user "bitbullbarbados" was quoted as saying:

"Man that new Trump video by TrumpCoinContent is incredible and high energy!!!
Superb job!"

AUGUST 2016

Titled "MAGA: Join The Fight For America", the full transcript of the video was the following. It was uploaded to YouTube on the 3rd of August:

> Donald Trump: "After four years of Hillary Clinton, what do we have? ISIS has spread across the region and the entire world. Libya is in ruins. We are a country that owes 19 trillion Dollars. We lose everywhere. We can't beat anybody. Our vets are being treated horribly."
>
> Hillary Clinton: "What difference at this point does it make?"
>
> Donald Trump: "These problems can all be fixed, but not by Hillary Clinton. Only by me."
>
> ...SONG (Stand Tall For The Beast Of America)...
>
> Donald Trump: "It will change. We will have so much winning if I get elected that you may get bored with winning. I agree, you will never get bored with winning, we never get bored..."
>
> ...SONG (Stand Tall For The Beast Of America)...

This video played for two minutes and eighteen seconds. It concluded by displaying a message which read:

> "Be a part of the people-funded causecoin initiative to help make America secure/safe/honest/strong/proud/free/rich/equal/successful/great."

On the 5th of August at 08:52:49 UTC, user "Skirmant" said:

> "I launched a Reddit tipbot if anyone is interested:
>
> https://www.reddit.com/r/trumpcoin/comments/4w9h91/trumpcoin_tipbot_is_live_umagatip
>
> Reply to the thread and you'll get a decent tip. Also, make sure to upvote, the bot NEEDS karma."

AUGUST 2016

On the 7th of August at 07:10:47 UTC, user "bitbullbarbados" said:

> "TrumpCoin Promotion Tokens
>
> I've recently made arrangements with a promotions company to produce some TrumpCoin marketing tokens!! This is a great way to tell the TrumpCoin story plus give out a symbolic TrumpCoin that can direct them to further info about buying TrumpCoins, etc.
>
> The front side is the Trump image along with the "In Trump We Trust" wording. The backside top has the text " Make America Great Again" , with a QR code in the center that points to the www.trumpcoin.com website. And the bottom text of www.trumpcoin.com for those that might not have a smartphone available but can at least know the address to lookup in a browser.
>
> The coins are made of a hard plastic and are very close to the size of a standard poker chip. The colored images and text are a hard plastic ink. These are super durable and are a great way to get the word out about our campaign promotion, future 'causes' and the TrumpCoin crypto story in general. A very easy way to educate friends, family, acquaintances and confused liberals about Trumpcoin!!
>
> I am giving these away in batches of 50 or 100. Please PM me with your request as well as shipping address. BitBullBarbados
> COST & SHIPPING:
> Any donation of Trumpcoin to: TU19bGSehkvN7LuqeLD11cfnSYp2tUhMH6
> Or Any donation of Bitcoin to: 1AVhG1PtzYVkMCeVoFsmwh5LCUmWgBPYF7
>
> MAGA !"

On the 12th of August at 13:23:55 UTC, user "Signal7" praised everyone who had contributed to the coin both publicly and behind closed doors. He also had a message for all supporters of TrumpCoin who were eagerly waiting for significant news. He promised a major update before the end of the month:

> "For legal and marketing reasons, I cannot disclose a whole lot just yet, but your wait is almost over. Within the next two weeks, we will be finally releasing all that has been happening behind the scenes and moving forward full throttle in our mission to help Donald Trump to Make America Great Again!"

AUGUST 2016

A few minor updates were announced by user "Signal7" on the 12th of August in order to keep members of the community engaged. These were:

> "New promotional videos: We have a few more videos coming very soon. Our next release is a bit of a fun little instructional for newbies to show them how to easily enter TrumpCoin.
>
> Signature Campaign: Active now. If we see a TrumpCoin wallet address in your signature here or anywhere else, we will tip you. The bigger and more creative your TrumpCoin signature is, the more coins you will get. If you need help creating a signature, please ask us here. We are more than happy to help.
>
> BTCT New Wallet Bonuses: BitcoinTalk members with non-newbie status are now eligible for free coins. To qualify, you must be a member of this forum with a status of Junior Member or better and not have a history of posting in any of the TrumpCoin threads to date. All that we ask in return is for you to download and evaluate our wallet or daemon and tell us about your experience here.
>
> Tips, Tips, Tips: Community contributors will begin receiving more consistent tips from the TrumpCoin Team. The Contributor Tipping Program will begin on Monday.
>
> Translation Bounties: Coming within the next 2 weeks. We must finalize the OP before moving forward with this. Once the final copy is ready, we will announce bounties for the languages that we need translations for.
>
> Flash Mob Fun: You should already be noticing various members of the TrumpCoin Team ramping up in social media and troll boxes. Keep an eye out for opportunities for free coins from trivias and other quick little promotions that are liable to come from virtually anywhere. These are flash campaigns and will not generally be announced in advance. These campaigns typically pay participants and even random passers by in one form or another."

On the 19th of August, an article was published titled "TrumpCoin Aims to Make Crypto Great Again". The full article can be found in the appendix of this book on pages 141 to 143.

Altcoin Today, the crypto news website that published the article, referred to the video uploaded by user "TrumpCoinContent" on the 7th of June. The opening segment of the article was:

> "A new currency — TrumpCoin — dedicated to supporting Donald Trump's presidency is currently seeking investments as a political action committee (PAC)."

On the 21st of August at 21:01:50 UTC, user "doogjy" said:

> "Hey all just got paid so I'm going through dropping some tips for those of you with addresses in your signature! I'll be doing this throughout the week, but make sure your address is valid because I've not been able to deposit in a few of them
>
> And if I see some new signatures that haven't been in this thread or posting much, they might get an outsized show of appreciation for their support!
>
> MAGA lads, I know things have been quiet but there was bound to be a lull as we move into place and make sure we get it right the first time, without false starts. Trust me, I'm excited too, but I've found in crypto a little patience can go a long way if you believe in the cause."

On the 24th of August at 18:36:40 UTC, user "Depredation" said:

> "A secondary block explorer will be working soon, once it has synced.
> Block explorer is online: https://www.blockexperts.com/trump
> Please give it a couple of hours to index all values."
> Just check up on it every few hours or so."

One user described an alternative block explorer as beneficial due to the fact that the one at http://chain.blockpioneers.info/trump/ was being problematic.

On the following day, the block explorer at https://www.blockexperts.com/trump had fully synced (caused to occur or operate at the same time or rate).

AUGUST 2016

On the 27th of August at 09:39:58 UTC, user "donarito" said:

> "emm, I guess today is one of the lowest trading volumes in TrumpCoin history 😔 quite sad fact actually.
>
> Long time no news from Signal. Dev team do you need some help from community?"

The number of updates and frequency of news related to the coin began to wane during the last week of August. As the month came to a close, user "Signal7" had not submitted a post (his last TrumpCoin Update) on the official TrumpCoin Bitcointalk thread since the 12th of August at 13:23:55 UTC. Throughout the entire month, user "Signal7" had posted sixteen times. His promise to disclose all that had been taking place behind the scenes did not occur. The community were very disappointed and began to shrink.

The last post of the month was on the 31st of August at 17:53:33 UTC. It was posted by user "donarito" who said:

> "any news from devs?"

Other events which occurred in the month of August were:

- On the 2nd of August, user "Signal7" was happy to announce that TrumpCoin had become powered in part by PayServices. It is an international organisation which provides a Multi Exchange Operating System [MEOS] and advanced APIs for seamless integrations into 3rd party storefronts. This had become the Trump Fund's new home and, from this point on, would be managed by the treasury.

- On the 17th of August, user "yaooke" uploaded his own TrumpCoin promotional video to YouTube at https://www.youtube.com/watch?v=uZ2w2g9tjCQ. Praise came from user "bitbullbarbados" who liked it very much.

AUGUST 2016

VENUES OF TRUMP'S SPEECHES

01/08	Town Hall	Columbus, OH
01/08	Rally	Mechanicsburg, PA
01/08	Rally	Harrisburg, PA
02/08	Rally	Ashburn, VA
03/08	Town Hall	Daytona Beach, FL
03/08	Rally	Jacksonville, FL
04/08	Rally	Portland, ME
05/08	Rally	Des Moines, IA
05/08	Rally	Green Bay, WI
08/08	Speech	Detroit, MI
09/08	Rally	Wilmington, NC
09/08	Rally	Fayetteville, NC
10/08	Speech	Abingdon, VA
10/08	Rally	Ft. Lauderdale, FL
11/08	Speech	Orlando, FL
11/08	Rally	Kissimmee, FL
12/08	Rally	Erie, PA
12/08	Rally	Altoona, PA
13/08	Rally	Fairfield, CT
15/08	Speech	Youngstown, OH
16/08	Speech	West Bend, OH
18/08	Rally	Charlotte, NC
19/08	Rally	Dimondale, MI
20/08	Rally	Fredericksburg, VA
22/08	Rally	Akron, OH
23/08	Rally	Austin, TX
24/08	Rally	Tampa, FL
24/08	Rally	Jackson, MS
25/08	Rally	Manchester, NH
27/08	Event	Des Moines, IA
30/08	Rally	Everett, WA
31/08	Speech	Phoenix, AZ

On the 31st of August, Republican Presidential Nominee Donald J. Trump and the President of Mexico Enrique Peña Nieto held a press conference.

HIGH RISKS ATTRIBUTED TO DONATING THE TRUMP FUND TO A POLITICAL CAMPAIGN

SEPTEMBER 2016

I. Progress announcements had become negligible in number.

II. User "DreadLordColi" resigned from the development team.

III. Two posts were submitted by user "Signal7" during the entire month.

IV. Members of the community began to post Trump related memes/bounties.

V. A TrumpCoin Twitter TipBot was created by user "Skirmant".

During the first few days of September, it was evident that announcements about the progress of the coin, both legally in terms of the LLC and socially, had become close to negligible. A substantial number of supporters of the coin began to question whether the development team had lost interest. Nevertheless, there were still individuals who still had faith in the TrumpCoin Project.

The Bitcoin Satoshi values of one unit of TRUMP account on YoBit and C-Cex were:

	Price	Low	Open	Close	High	Volume (TRUMP)
1st Sept (YB)	8,855	8,173	9,000	8,710	9,212	20,659.82
1st Sept (CC)	8,642	7,160	8,384	8,900	8,900	33,972.95

source: www.cryptocompare.com

SEPTEMBER 2016

On the 9th of September at 13:33:43 UTC, user "DreadLordColi" announced:

> "Hi all. Just wanted to chime in and make a quick two part announcement about TrumpCoin and my involvement in it.
>
> For starters; I am currently no longer part of the TrumpCoin development team in any capacity after this post and have stepped down as treasurer of the project indefinitely. From this point forward I will be returning to my original "role" as simply a fan/investor and will no longer be privy to an inside information. My original plan was to only be treasurer on an interim basis, in what I felt was a time of need for the project. During my stint as treasurer and "SEO guy" - I took zero salary, received no donations and spent my own fiat on any promotion I did for the coin - I hope this reputation will follow me in the cryptocurrency community going forward, as that is what I love about crypto most; the community.
>
> That being said...
>
> I will gladly monopolize the attention and add that, the reason I am stepping down is to:
>
> a) focus on my own little crypto endeavors :^) and
> b) because I am being replaced by someone infinitely more qualified who will be able to take this project to lengths we originally only dreamt were possible.
>
> With this person in the chair, I feel like media attention is possible if we market the pac immediately after :^).
>
> I'll let someone from the official dev team fill you in on all the particulars, but let's just say the new treasurer has done this SPECIFIC task before and is professionally someone that "you better call" - hint hint.
>
> I'd like to thank everyone who sent me an email or a PM recently, showing support or just looking to chat; please feel free to continue doing so!
>
> That's it from me for now,
> See you around the boards!
> - Colin"

Both users "Bitbobb" and "Signal7" thanked him for his hard work, help and service towards TrumpCoin. They wished him luck in all his future endeavours.

SEPTEMBER 2016

After just over four weeks, user "Signal7" posted on the official TrumpCoin Bitcointalk thread on the 9th of September at 16:01:11 UTC. He said that he had had some important personal business to catch up with over those few weeks. He assured the community that he was still active in TrumpCoin and had just caught up with all the events which had occurred. He also was quoted as saying:

> "The 100k that was sent to me is still staking here:
> TSt65isKg47WXPEXa7Rq866QCTNxYFL2CB
>
> I have put a ton of research into how we can and cannot use this money and what we can and cannot do as far as Super PACs are concerned. Turns out, we can do a lot more than we originally thought and we can actually cause some very significant changes at the federal level for the benefit of crypto - ALL cryptos - through our cause.
>
> I understand that many are anxious, I still need a few more days before a real announcement."

As a consequence of the above, confidence in the community began to show signs of recovery. There were still people who wanted something more concrete from user "Signal7" instead of vague announcements. There were two pages (forty posts) of content during the first nine days of September. At this time, the following four exchanges still offered trading of TrumpCoin:

On the 15th of September at 22:39:16 UTC, user "Bitbobb" said:

> "Signal has the super pac getting formed with an attorney. And he has some personal business he is juggling. He is still getting things done behind the scenes relative to the PAC."

123

SEPTEMBER 2016

On the 16th of September at 15:44:04 UTC, user "Signal7" posted his second and final comment during September. The opening part of the announcement was:

> "I know you all are chomping at the bit for news. Please understand that the legal side of what we are doing is extremely complex and I am placing myself in a position of very high risk, both legally and financially.
>
> We are at a critical stage currently and I have to be extremely careful about what I say and how I present myself.
>
> There are three specific goals that are attached to this project:
> 1. Promote Donald Trump for President in the best way we can
> 2. Promote Crooked Hillary for Prison in the best way we can
> 3. Donate cryptocurrency to Trump's campaign, which actually requires us to advance cryptocurrency support and acceptance in U.S. government, starting with the FEC."

He stressed the fact that the Trump Fund could not be used in anyway in relation to FEC (Federal Election Commission) guidelines. As a result, it could not be legally donated to any political campaign or PAC due to the fact the fund was handed to user "Signal7" by user "chicken65" who is foreign national. Therefore, user "Signal7" said he was potentially at risk of criminal charges if he went ahead with any donations. Alternatively, the Trump Fund could definitely go towards funding social grassroots of TrumpCoin initiatives such as videos, explorers and so on.

A path forward had been chosen:

> "We are merging with BitPAC (http://www.bit-pac.com/). There will be a new Statement of Organization filed in the near future that lists me (Jason M. Bobbitt) as the new Treasurer and bylaws amended that list me as the new Executive Director. Dan Backer will remain listed as Asst. Treasurer and his legal firm will continue as an active vendor of BitPAC.
>
> BitPAC has already established itself as a force to be reckoned with. There will be some further advancements to the BitPAC that I cannot discuss openly just yet. The proposed changes will benefit TrumpCoin in some significant ways and pave the way for many/all other cryptos to follow suit."

As soon as user "Signal7" had said the Trump Fund could be used in social campaigns to promote the coin, there were suggestions floated on the official Trumpcoin Bitcointalk thread on how to proceed. One of these was put forward by user "Raexno" who posted the following:

> "Could the remainder of the trump fund be used towards paying for the coin to be on bittrex?
>
> Even part contributing towards it would be good. A more reputable exchange can only help."

User "Depredation" concurred. He viewed the post above as a great idea if TrumpCoin did not, over a long period, manage to get added naturally. He would be willing to donate his own money towards getting the coin added to Bittrex. He knew how important a more reputable exchange would be for the coin's image.

Also, an concerted effort was taking place to associate the coin with the "alt-right" movement and Pepe The Frog.

Two memes posted on the 22nd and 23rd of September were respectively:

SEPTEMBER 2016

On the 24th of September, user "Raexno" initiated a TrumpCoin bounty promotional campaign. It was an opportunity to earn TRUMP (from an originally raised fund of 6,000 TRUMP) by carrying out certain tasks. Users had to have a Twitter account with at least ten followers. Two promotional tasks given can be seen depicted on page 120.

On the following day at 00:02:56 UTC, user "Skirmant" announced that he had created a Twitter TipBot specifically for TrumpCoin. It was now possible for someone to send TRUMP to anyone on Twitter by including "#magatip x TRUMP" in the Tweet (x being the amount). He admitted that it was minimalistic, but was content it was working properly. It can be found at https://maga.vicenet.org.

Two days later, user "Bitbobb" told the community he had just sent "Diamond and Silk" and Alex Jones 50 TRUMPS each. As far as he knew, both accepted the tips.

```
Transactions:
You tipped IrritateBwoman (-2 TRUMP)
You tipped PrisonPlanet (-50 TRUMP)
You tipped LoveStephanysco (-10 TRUMP)
You tipped NubianAwakening (-20 TRUMP)
You tipped realstevemiis (-10 TRUMP)
You tipped DiamondandSilk (-50 TRUMP)
```

Also on the 27th of September, user "bitbullbarbados" gave out at least 1,000 TrumpCoin Promotional Tokens (see page 110) to supporters of Donald J. Trump at a rally in Melbourne, Florida. He stated the attendance at the rally as 25,000+ and was in awe of the spectacle. He actually said "This is a movement people!".

On the last day of the month, the Bitcoin Satoshi value of one unit of TRUMP account had decreased from its value on the 1st of September. YoBit and C-Cex were still the two major cryptocurrency exchanges on which the vast majority of trades of TRUMP were taking place:

	Price	Low	Open	Close	High	Volume (TRUMP)
30th Sept (YB)	5,517	4,830	4,830	6,204	7,249	21,842.65
30th Sept (CC)	6,381.5	5,350	5,513	7,250	7,264	64,997.79

source: www.cryptocompare.com

SEPTEMBER 2016

VENUES OF TRUMP'S SPEECHES

01/09	Rally	Wilmington, OH
03/09	Speech	Detroit, MI
06/09	Q&A	Virginia Beach, VA
06/09	Rally	Greenville, NC
07/09	Speech	Philadelphia, PA
08/09	Speech	Cleveland, OH
09/09	Speech	Washington, DC
09/09	Rally	Pensacola, FL
12/09	Speech	Baltimore, MD
12/09	Rally	Asheville, NC
13/09	Rally	Des Moines, IA
13/09	Speech	Aston, PA
14/09	Speech	Flint, MI
14/09	Rally	Canton, OH
15/09	Rally	Laconia, NH
16/09	Pres Conf	Washington, DC
16/09	Rally	Miami, FL
17/09	Rally	Colorado Springs, CO
19/09	Rally	Fort Myers, FL
20/09	Rally	High Point, NC
20/09	Rally	Kenansville, NC
21/09	Speech	Cleveland, OH
21/09	Rally	Toledo, OH
22/09	Rally	Chester Twp., PA
24/09	Rally	Roanoke, VA
26/09	Debate	Hempstead, NY
27/09	Rally	Melbourne, FL
28/09	Speech	Chicago, IL
28/09	Rally	Council Bluffs, IA
28/09	Rally	Waukesha, WI
29/09	Rally	Bedford, NH
30/09	Rally	Novi, MI

On the 26th of September, the first Presidential Debate occurred between Hillary Clinton and Donald J. Trump at Hofstra University in Hempstead, NY.

TrumpCoin—Make Crypto Great Again

EIGHT MONTHS OF TRUMPCOIN
OCTOBER 2016

I. A brief description of TrumpCoin was sent to the Breitbart News Network.

II. A Re-correcting The Record #RCTR campaign was encouraged on Twitter.

III. A promotional video was uploaded to YouTube by user "yaooke".

IV. User "chicken65" suggested how the project could move forward.

V. User "Signal7" had not logged into Bitcointalk since the 27th of September.

Once again, there had been prolonged silence from the lead developer. User "Signal7" had not posted on the official TrumpCoin Bitcointalk thread for two weeks since his last major update. Some members of the TrumpCoin Team reported that they had not been in contact with user "Signal7" for at least one month.

On the 3rd of October at 18:28:40 UTC, user "Bitbobb" said:

> "Things I can confirm: Yes reporter from Breitbart is asking for info on what is Trumpcoin. Yes shapeshift will include us once this coin meets their criteria for inclusion to their platform
>
> Things I need: A rough draft article for the reporter to review to intro them to trumpcoin. Is there anyone willing to write out some notes or a rough article on trumpcoin? I am looking for an Android programmer please pm me with info."

OCTOBER 2016

On the following day, according to user "Raexno", user "Bitbobb" sent a brief description of what TrumpCoin is to Breitbart. The Breitbart News Network is a politically conservative American news website founded in 2007.

On the 5th of October at 14:20:02 UTC, user "TrumpCoinContent" said:

> "Hey guys
>
> Apologise for the radio silence, been very busy working on content for both the TC channel and other personal business.
>
> Shy of video work there's not much else I can contribute but have a line-up of videos soon to be released (essentially anti-hillary/pro-trump campaign advertisement with a "paid for by trumpcoin" featured at the end) as well as an instructional.
>
> When they do drop feel free to spread them literally anywhere, they're going to be considerably more inflammatory than Trump himself is allowed to get away with so my thinking is we can operate as his deniability attack dog.
>
> Feel free to make any suggestions as I'm about to start dropping quite a lot of content that the media seems hesitant on packaging."

As mentioned in the quote above, user "TrumpCoinContent", the current media content manager of TrumpCoin, acknowledged he was still part of the official TrumpCoin Team and was only working on video content, nothing else. He told the community to expect a video within the next week.

Also on the 5th of October, user "Bitbobb" posted the following billboard:

On the 10th of October at 00:55:15 UTC, user "Bitbobb" said:

> "20 minute warning. If you have twitter you can accept the #magatip twitter bot https://maga.vicenet.org/index.php and send TRUMPcoins to people on Twitter whom you like to support. A community member has called this Re-correcting the record #RCTR and I have used the twitter bot to hand out over 900 TRUMPcoins.
>
> If you will like to donate to the official twitter account here is the address to directly send trumpcoin to it: TGdShj7r7NFAzDFhuP8akuEMmUfzBtv6Me
>
> Each Trumpcoin there will be sent out during this debate.
>
> I encourage each of you to RCTR live on twitter. Trump has a group he has asked to do this. Another group called Nible America is doing this and then there is us. I think we are the only "group" that provides a financial reward of sorts to correct the record. So we are unique. Do not miss this chance to be a part of history."

During the next couple of days, user "manhunterBTC" kept persistently posting large font remarks and obscene comments on the official Bitcointalk thread.

On the 12th of October at 08:43:15 UTC, user "yaooke" said:

> "Here is a new video:
>
> https://www.youtube.com/watch?v=8Ksjp7p-aDM"

This was the second promotional TrumpCoin video created by user "yaooke". It was titled "Donald Trump - The Alpha Male" and lasts two minutes and one second. His first video was uploaded to YouTube on the 17th of August 2016.

Despite the absence of user "Signal7", members of the community were still participating and contributing to the coin.

OCTOBER 2016

On the 14th of October at 13:37:18 UTC, user "chicken65" said:

> "Hi folks.
>
> First, forget signal, the Trump fund and anyone else that championed the hostile takeover of Trump Coin which undoubtedly was severly damaging to this coins trajectory. I still have my half of the Trump fund which will never be used (of course I will prove this). I repeat - That fund will never be sold off......**in this current cyle of the coin.**
>
> Now, that brings me to something else. Ive been working on what I consider to be a game changer in Crypto. In fact the truth is Ive been working on it ever since the beginning of Trump Coin which was intended to be an experience driven project for me (was never about $$$). This new project could be helpful to Trump Coin (very helpful). It would mean another coin swap but the features of the new coin would be truly awesome. Wouldnt be happening in the next few weeks, just floating the idea out there to you guys.
>
> In terms of my interests in Trump Coin - I am completely out except for the 100k Fund which will never be sold. Im merely suggesting I might be able to help extend the life of the coin and it will be on a completely new blockchain design with features that floors all the competition. The new version of TC on this new blockchain would be very good for its prospects.
>
> And if we do this I would want us to start using the original thread again. This one was low energy, zero fun, and reeked of heavy duty corporate and even PC - the exact opposite of what the Trump movement is about. If its a no go then thats fine by me also."

On the following day, user "chicken65" suggested that TrumpCoin should further strengthen its ties with the "alt-right" movement. He believed there was still life in the TrumpCoin project.

On the 17th of October, user "Signal7" had not posted on the official TrumpCoin Bitcointalk thread since the beginning of the month and had not logged into the forum for three weeks. Also on this day at 19:56:31 UTC, user "chicken65" said:

> "Not me I believe he will win. Hes way ahead in the ramussen polls. Establishment lying polls cannot be trusted.
> They did the same with Brexit, At one point remain were supposed to be 14 points ahead."

OCTOBER 2016

VENUES OF TRUMP'S SPEECHES

01/10	Speech	Manheim, PA
03/10	Town Hall	PAC Event
03/10	Rally	Pueblo, CO
03/10	Rally	Loveland, CO
04/10	Rally	Prescott Valley, AZ
05/10	Rally	Henderson, NV
05/10	Rally	Neno, NV
06/10	Town Hall	Sandown, NH
09/10	Debate	St. Louis, MO
10/10	Rally	Ambridge, PA
10/10	Rally	Wilkes-Barre, PA
11/10	Rally	Panama City, FL
12/10	Rally	Ocala, FL
12/10	Rally	Lakeland, FL
13/10	Rally	West Palm Beach, FL
13/10	Rally	Columbus, OH
13/10	Rally	Cincinnati, OH
14/10	Rally	Greensboro, NC
14/10	Rally	Charlotte, NC
15/10	Rally	Portsmouth, NH
15/10	Rally	Bangor, ME
17/10	Rally	Green Bay, WI

On the 9th of October, the Second Presidential Debate took place between Hillary Clinton and Donald J. Trump at Washington University in St. Louis, MO.

On the 19th of October, the Third (Final) Presidential Debate took place between Hillary Clinton and Donald J. Trump at University of Nevada, Las Vegas, NV.

APPENDIX

VOCATIV ARTICLE TITLED "INTRODUCING TRUMPCOIN, THE CURRENCY FOR FANS OF DONALD TRUMP" PUBLISHED ON THE 6TH OF APRIL 2016

Introducing TrumpCoin, The Currency For Fans Of Donald Trump

"One Scottish Trump fan created a cryptocurrency honouring the presidential candidate.

(Photo Illustration: R. A. Di Ieso)

Donald Trump supporters who have resisted using Bitcoin because it wasn't stamped with their preferred presidential candidate no longer have an excuse.

TrumpCoin is here.

It's the latest in a never-ending stream of alternate cryptocurrencies, or altcoins, which function similarly to Bitcoin: They work in theory like a currency, are "mined" by computers working on an algorithm and are stored on user accounts called wallets. Hundreds of altcoins compete for users' attention at any given time, and while the user experience is similar for each, it's not uncommon for an altcoin to adopt a familiar face. Dogecoin, named for the "doge" meme, is still widely traded. The ill-fated Coinye West, on the other hand, shut down after being sued by Kanye West. Trump, as it happens, holds a certain appeal for believers in a radically free market economy.

TrumpCoin's founder identifies himself only by the username Chicken65—like a much of the cryptocurrency world, he's reluctant to use his real name—but told Vocativ in a Skype interview that he's a Scottish music producer, bald and around 40 years old. Like many in the cryptocurrency world, he's a longtime fan of free markets and opponent of government regulation of the financial world, and feels Donald Trump is the highest profile representation of those ideas in the world today.

"In my ideal world there would be no such thing as governments, banks, welfare states, institutionalized education, nationalized heathcare and so on," Chicken65 said. "I don't agree with all [Trump] says," he wrote, "but I couldn't call the coin 'The Free Society Logic Reason Truth and Philosophical coin.'" He notes that has come with its own set of problems. "[T]he coin has been under attack from day one" from people trying to knock it offline with DDoS attacks, he says—"some people seem to like attacking anything Trump."

Like all but a handful of altcoins, an individual TrumpCoin is practically worthless at the moment, with market watch site Coinmarketcap listing one TrumpCoin as worth about $0.005. But it's only two months old, and Chicken65 has big plans for TrumpCoin—he plans to soon upgrade it to Version 2, which comes with a host of new features. But even if it never takes off, it's not just as much about the money, he says—it's also about reminding people that economic freedom can mean freedom from government-sponsored currency.

"I believe we don't need any form of government … generally all state institutions practice violence against their populations. Taxation is a form of violence," Chicken65 said. "I simply don't understand why people love government—they are terrorists. They have killed the vast majority of people in human history. They are our enemy."

ALTCOIN TODAY ARTICLE TITLED "TRUMPCOIN AIMS TO MAKE CRYPTO GREAT AGAIN" PUBLISHED ON THE 19TH OF AUGUST 2016

TrumpCoin Aims to Make Crypto Great Again

A new currency—TrumpCoin—dedicated to supporting Donald Trump's presidency is currently seeking investments as a political action committee (PAC).

Support Trump 'Without Giving Away All Your Money'

TrumpCoin, which calls itself "the world's first cryptopac", even launched an updated website in its latest incarnation, which features an instructional video on its aims. "Let's make crypto great again", the closing slogan of the video drones. It describes TrumpCoun as "a way you could support the Trump campaign without giving away all your money".

The website states TrumpCoin is unaffiliated with Trump and has no official connections to anything surrounding his official presidential campaign. Users are referred to the coin's Bitcointalk thread for in-depth information.

The setup behind the coin appears familiar enough. A total of 6 million TrumpCoins are available for purchase, with 200,000 of these se aside in a so-called "Trump Fund", which will be donated to Trump's campaign in USD "once it reaches a substantial value", the video explains.

TrumpCoins' value overall is stated to increase from heightened demand through marketing, allowing alleged profits to be dished out to investors and forwarded to Trump as donations.

The language employed throughout the official site and video is tellingly basic in order to interest, one Reddit user suggests, a maximum cross-section of non-technical investors.

"The best part is unlike a donation where you never see your money again, when you buy TrumpCoins you now own those TrumpCoins", the latter continues. The screen depicts a cash donation to the Clinton Foundation, which is marked as a "scam".

A browse through the TrumpCoin Bitcointalk thread however produces a feeling of foreboding. Navigating away from the page chosen as the linking destination from the TrumpCoin website, one quickly encounters infighting developers and disarray, which are grimly familiar to those of countless other niche altcoins.

"Just as I suspected [developer] Signal7 isn't prepared to send the coins in to Escrow" a post by developer Chris Cowie reads. "That man's sole objective when he sneaked his way into this project was to sell of his coins totalling more than 2 million which he mined using the computers in the data centre he works at. Everything he has done has been about that, nothing more".

Cowie also accuses Signal7 of "wanting to steal" the Trump Fund. More than that, however, the thread is in fact locked. The last message is from Cowie, who states that as of July he has "no choice but to lock this thread for good". "As time goes on the fud will just become more and more", he concluded.

While TrumpCoin is already the subject of predictable debate, and listed at around $0.05 on CoinMarketCap, investors lured by the latest website will quickly unearth the kind of activity from Bitcointalk alone that points to a less-than-solid operation in which to invest personal funds.

Would you buy TrumpCoin to support Donald Trump's campaign? Let us know in the comments section below!

www.ingramcontent.com/pod-product-compliance
Lightning Source LLC
LaVergne TN
LVHW021108190125
801668LV00035B/1237